The Way It Is

"Corbin Harney stands as no one else does at the moment for that new alliance between indigenous peoples and environmental groups. I see him in the coming years as a very prominent figure in the global movement that eventually, I hope, will prevent major catastrophes from happening.

"If we are to survive the decade of the nineties, I firmly believe people have to take action. People have to wake up and heed the call of the Corbin Harneys, the Bill Rosses, the Kazakhs, and Pacific Islanders.

"The Corbin Harneys of the world advance no hidden political agenda. They speak from the heart—basic, genuine, sincere. They speak from experience, and they speak, unfortunately, as witnesses to incredible human suffering. I think this indigenous voice could be described as the conscience of our planet."

—Stephan Dompke, Director,
Society for a Nuclear-Free Future, Berlin

"What Corbin talks about is so basic and so real . . . when he calls it Mother Earth and he talks about the land—it's so basic. It's just the way it is. It's not any high-tech anything; it's just basic living and life. He puts everything in perspective and gives everybody a sense of why they're here, and, like the burning in the heart, he gives you a renewed feeling that maybe you can make a difference."

—Claudia Peterson, St. George, Utah

"Our land is suffering on account of nuclear testing and
uranium mining. We have to preserve this Earth.
We rely on this Earth to give us food, clothing, and all the luxury
that we have. Everything is here for us to use,
but nuclear energy is not the way to continue with what we have.
We don't understand radiation or
how the release of nuclear energy is affecting the Earth.
Our forefathers didn't know anything about it,
and our medicine people don't know how to cure people from it.

Photo: Linda Putnam

All Nations Healing Ceremony
Nevada Test Site, April 1991

"The Mother Earth provides us with food,
provides us with air, provides us with water.
We, the people, are going to have to put our thoughts together,
our power together, to save our planet here.
We've only got one water, one air, one Mother Earth."

The Way It Is

One Water . . .
One Air . . .
One Mother Earth . . .

Corbin Harney

SPIRITUAL LEADER
OF THE
WESTERN SHOSHONE NATION

Blue Dolphin Publishing
1995

Published by Blue Dolphin Publishing, Inc.
P.O. Box 8, Nevada City, CA 95959. Orders: 1-800-643-0765
Web: http://www.bluedolphinpublishing.com

Thanks to all of the people and organizations listed in the text and
appendix for permission to use source material in this book, especially Idaho Public Television for providing additional interviews
with the author in preparation for their program: "One Water. One
Air. One Mother Earth."

Special thanks to all the photographers who contributed freely of
their work: Nancy and Paul Clemens, Scott Foglesong, Hawkeye
Haven, James Lerager, Paul John Miller/Black Star, Will Powers,
Linda Putnam, Sabine Sauer/Lichtblick Fotografie, and Dan True.

And to all the people over the years making audio recordings,
videotapes, interviewing, transcribing, compiling, and editing,
sincere thanks.

This book is gratefully published in part with grants from the
Foundation for a Compassionate Society, Kyle, Texas, and from the
Chapel of St. Francis, Shundahai Network, Nevada City, California.

Library of Congress Cataloging-in-Publication Data

Harney, Corbin, 1920–
    The way it is : one water, one air, one mother earth / by Corbin Harney.
        p. cm.
    Includes index.
    ISBN 0-931892-80-5
    1. Shoshoni Indians—Religion.   2. Indians of North America—
Religion.   3. Human ecology—Religious aspects.
I. Title.
E99.S4H27 1995
299'.784—dc20   94-35900
                                                             CIP

Cover design: Lito Castro
Front cover photo: Hawkeye Haven

Printed in the United States of America
9   8   7   6   5   4   3   2

Dedicated

to Mother Earth
who gives us life through the Creator
who gives us our water, our food, our medicine

to the One Spirit
to the eagle, buffalo, and bear
who have helped me on the path
and given me strength

to all the living things
in the circle of life

to the well-being of the elders, the young
and all future generations

that all beings have a good life
and continue on

Shundahai

Corbin: "A lot of things we don't understand, but the Spirit is the one that carries them. The Spirit tells them where to go or how to do. The Spirit tells the people what to get, where to go. Today we think, well, it's just luck if something good happens. It's not luck. It's the Spirit telling us, guiding us all the way!"

Contents

Foreword

Corbin Harney is our spiritual leader. He's also one of our doctors, one who takes care of us when we're sick. He's able to heal us of different ailments. We always depended on doctors like Corbin before modern medicine came in. Now I guess we have to depend on modern medicine instead of our own medicine. If they catch Corbin doctoring, they might try to lock him up because he doesn't have an M.D. or a Ph.D. behind his name, but we all know he's a doctor.

You have to really believe in this way in order for one of our doctors to be able to heal you—and they *can* heal you. They have the methods. In other words, if you go to them and say, "You can't heal me," then it won't take effect. The Native people believe in their healer, and they don't have to go in front of these x-ray machines to find out what's wrong with them. I have been healed by some healers. A couple of times I took off without my medication, went down in a canyon looking for Corbin. When I wound up there without any medication and started hurting

Corbin Harney and Bill Rosse, Sr.

pretty bad, finally I had Corbin work on me, and then I felt fine. It kept me going until I could get medication.

He's the one who does all the praying. He prays to the Creator for everything that's put here on Earth, and he prays for us—prays *with* us, asks *us* to pray, asks us to give our offering. See, our belief is that whenever you take something away from Mother Earth, you put something back, you exchange for it. That's the way we keep balance in Mother Earth, by taking and giving.

Corbin does the praying for us, daily, for our bodies, so we depend on him very much. We're working with the younger children, because we have a lot of problems with drugs, alcohol, and different things. We try to bring the children out to the spiritual and healing ceremonies, several times a year. When the young people get out in nature, they clean up pretty well, but as soon as they get back home, they tend to continue the way they were going before, and it's a long time between gatherings.

Corbin and the other elders look out for us all and try to keep us on the right path. This is such an important thing, because we're losing a lot of the old people; they're getting too old, and nobody really has wanted to take their place. We are working to inspire the young people to carry on the tradition, to learn all they can about our spiritual ways.

Even though Corbin and I are leaders in name, we—all of us—share environmental responsibility to be in charge of this Earth. The Bible tells you to be a steward of this land, which means that you take care of what's here. The Creator created all this for us, created us and all that's here with us, perfectly. Humans started thinking that because of their technology they are a bit better than the Creator, trying to move things around to suit themselves that the Creator put in certain places, and this is a mistake. We're paying for it with the ozone being eaten away and the depletion of our resources. We need to use all our resources sparingly and always return something back to Mother Earth to give her the energy to keep going and add more to it.

In my understanding from working with Corbin, our Native people's religion is like the Old Testament. The Natives don't understand Jesus Christ's coming, but they do know there was a Creator who created all of this, and they give thanks for that. They thank the Creator for taking care of all the things that are here and for seeing that they continue on.

The Natives don't go to church: the whole Mother Earth in the open air is our church; we stay out in the open. In our own way, we go to church daily. When we go stand out here just before sunrise, we're standing there when that sun comes up, and we wash ourselves in that sunlight and bless ourselves and ask the Creator's blessing on us, and that He keep us going.

The essence of the Native religion is the Spirit, the spiritual part of us, our faith that the Creator made us, and that He'll promise us a good place to go after our lives if we do the work that He asks us to do. This is what keeps Corbin and I on the ball, and is the basis of our work. We're not perfect, but we're trying to do what the Creator sets out for us to do.

Bill Rosse, Sr.
Chairman, Environmental Protection Committee,
Western Shoshone National Council*

Note:
*Bill Rosse, Sr., passed away in 1999. He did well what the Creator set out for him to do.

Introduction

Corbin Harney is an elder and spiritual leader of the Western Shoshone, a Native people indigenous to Idaho, Nevada, Utah, and California. Born in Idaho, his mother died a few hours after his birth, and he was raised by medicine people of the Owyhee Indian reservation. Since 1957 he has worked with Eunice Silva and Florence Vega, medicine women of Battle Mountain, Nevada, running the Sundance Ceremony, sweat lodges, and doctoring sick people. As a medicine person, he has also been working steadily to preserve and protect the sacred sites and burial grounds of his people. In addition, he has been instrumental in helping to stop nuclear testing on Shoshone land at the Nevada Test Site.

When Corbin leads people in prayer inside the traditional sweat lodge, he beats his drum, the heartbeat of the Mother Earth, and sings medicine songs in his native Shoshone language. Without knowing the language, many people who have been inside the sweat lodge feel the power of the prayers and emerge feeling "renewed," "cleared," "blessed," or "healed."

When asking Corbin about his prayers, he translates simply, saying that he is praying to the Earth . . . praying that it can be saved from the pollution and radiation that is destroying the balance of nature and hurting the humans, animals, plant life, the air, the rocks, and the water. He makes prayers that all of us be able to have enough food and water and good air . . . and that this abundance be safeguarded for future generations. He prays for the animals, the plants, the mountains, the waterways . . . nothing is forgotten.

"A few years ago I was praying to the water," Corbin said. "I was praying that it would run pure and clear, and that it would be able to take care of us for countless generations. The water came to me and spoke to me. It said: 'In a few years I'm going to look like water, but you're not going to be able to use me anymore.'"

Corbin told this story to us, saying that it was a few years ago when he had this vision. Now he feels the day is here. Much of our water throughout the world is already contaminated. Corbin is deeply saddened by the state of the Earth, especially the damage he sees coming from the underground nuclear testing that goes on sixty miles northwest of Las Vegas on Western Shoshone land. "Nuclear testing has forced radioactivity into our water table. It is just a matter of time before all the water becomes contaminated if we don't put a stop to this nuclear testing."

In 1863 the Peace and Friendship Treaty of Ruby Valley was signed between the Shoshone and the U.S. government. This treaty honored particular lands as belonging to the Shoshone with permission granted to U.S. citizens to cross the land undisturbed in their migration west.

In 1951 President Harry Truman illegally seized the land for use by government agencies, primarily the Department of Energy. This broken treaty has not yet been conclusively tested in court, and for the last forty years the Shoshone have been fighting to reclaim these lands which they feel still belong to them.

Corbin Harney "came out from behind the bush," as he says, and in 1985 started to protest the U.S. government's nuclear weapons testing. Along with other Western Shoshone leaders, they crossed the cattleguard onto the 1,350-square-mile Test Site. Soon they were joined by more and more people in marches supporting a nuclear test ban.

As an advocate for the well-being of our Mother Earth, Corbin has taken hundreds of protestors into the sweat lodge in order to pray. He has always encouraged a strong but peaceful demonstration. As the years went by, more and more demonstrators have been coming to the Test Site. Some have chosen to be arrested, and others come to support the movement without crossing over the cattleguard.

In addition to U.S. citizens, people from all over the world have attended these gatherings, and the international sector— from Kazakhstan, England, Germany, France, Sweden, Belgium, Netherlands, India, Australia, Japan, and elsewhere—is notably represented at the Test Site. Corbin has said many times, "We all breathe the same air . . . all over this world. We all drink the same water. We are all warmed by the same sun, and we are all fed and nourished by the same Earth. What we do here in Nevada affects the life of everyone on the planet."

There is evidence that the underground tests do leak radiation above ground. "Down-winders," people who live downwind from the Test Site, especially those in southern Utah, have observed extremely high numbers of cancers, leukemia, and other physical deformities in their population. They feel sure that these alarming incidences of illness come from exposure to radiation from the Nuclear Test Site. Citizens in Kazakhstan (in the former Soviet Union) who lived downwind from a nearby test site have reported the same high levels of cancer, leukemia, illness, and birth deformities. Their protest was so fervent and well organized that they were successful in having their test site shut down.

But a grim reminder of their test site remains. In 1993 when Corbin visited Kazakhstan, he learned that the water is irreversibly contaminated with dangerous levels of radiation. "You can't drink a glass of water there anymore," Corbin said. "All they had to drink was Vodka, cartons of juice, and bottled water imported from Europe."

At a visit to a children's hospital, Corbin prayed for children who were suffering from birth deformities and painful, terminal illnesses caused by radiation poisoning. "This is really sad," he said, "because these people are going through what is soon coming our way. We've got to wake up and do something about it. The contamination is still going on today, and soon it's going to be too late. How can we live on without water? How can anything live?"

When he spoke at the Glastonbury Festival in England (spring 1994), he said, "I was told that raw nuclear waste is being dumped into the Irish Sea covering 300 square miles. This is terrible! That water travels everywhere, and the contamination is already destroying our sea life . . . and without our sea life, how can we live on? It is time for all of us, wherever we are, to start working together to save our planet here.

"Everywhere I go, people say, 'But, what can I do about this? I'm just one person. It's too big to stop because our economy is based largely on things that pollute our Earth.'"

Corbin responds, "All these things, like the nuclear plants and test sites, the mining toxins and chemical plants are all destroying our Earth. We're sucking our mother dry. If we want to have a Mother Earth to leave to our future generations, then we have to stop the way we're doing things now. The only way, as I see it, is to return to a native way of life where we take care of everything that we've got. From the beginning of time, that was the native way.

"In my life as a native of the land, I have tried to preserve our sacred sites and burial grounds. I have tried to keep our culture alive among the young people. These things are important. But now the very survival of all life is at stake, and we must save our Earth before we don't have an Earth to live on anymore.

"We, the people today, everywhere across this Mother Earth, need to unite together, no matter what color we are, no matter what 'lango' we speak. We need to find ways to get involved to help our Mother. Take pictures and videos to show what's going on. There is power in the people when we unite together. There is an even greater power when we come together to pray for our Mother Earth and all the living things. I always say, 'Don't pray like me; pray your own way, but pray for everything out there.' Everything is alive and we forget that. Prayer is the only way we're going to live on.

"The Spirit came to me and said, 'You're going to have to come out from behind the bush and give us a hand here.' But not just me. Now it's time for all of us to come out from behind the bush. You people, you have a voice. Use that voice! Let's work together to have a beautiful, clean Earth for our future generations."

Nancy and Paul Clemens
Blue Dolphin Publishing, Inc.

What I Stand For

Why I Am a Spiritual Teacher

To a certain extent, I am a spiritual person, a healer, because my blood is that way. I was born with that kind of blood, and I can't get away from it. I've been trying to teach the young people how to take care of themselves if they're born to be healers, if they're gifted people. So far it's been very hard, because even though it's something they know about, they still don't want to use their gifts. I know, because I've been through those feelings myself.

As Indian people, we're shy. We don't want to do anything out there in the world unless we're really up against it. I was sick a couple of times and was told by the Indian doctors that I have to follow what the Spirit tells me to do. See, I wasn't following those instructions for a while, and so I got sick. Then after somebody else told me what this sickness was about, from then on I came out from behind the bush and started doing what I'm doing today.

What I'm doing is praying for people, running sweats, trying to teach our young people what we should be doing in order for us to pass on a healthier life for the next, the younger generation.

I knew I was gifted as a healer right from the beginning when I was very young, when I realized that I could see sickness in people. I could understand their thinking—whatever it was they were thinking, I could pick it up in the air—and what they were saying. Even from quite a distance away, I could still hear what they were saying and thinking. That's how I knew I was gifted, but I didn't want to tell anybody about it. Just one time I told my uncle what I saw in one person, the sickness I saw in him.

He told me, "That's what you saw, but don't tell me. That's your gift, not mine. Don't tell me about it. But you are going to go through the same thing I've been through." That's what I was told by my uncle, who was also gifted.

You see, all gifted people are born with it. They're not taught it from a book. They didn't go to school for it or read up on it. It was just naturally given to them, and some people have a very strong gift.

So that's how we have healers, and that gift is among all of us—not only among the Indian people, but also out among the white man—those are the ones who have the power to heal you, by touching you, praying for you, or however.

Some of the animals are healers, too. Some birds are healers: that's why Indian people really understand and try to connect with the eagle. The eagle is very important to Indians for healing, for doctoring, and so forth, because the eagle is a very wise bird. He understands; he talks to people, and so forth. A healing place like our canyon at Rock Creek (in northern Nevada), with the eagle head medicine rock right there, is part of all that. All these things are connected together. We people have cured sickness for thousands of years using these healing places and our natural gifts, and it is very important that we continue to do so. That's the reason I'm saying to my young people, if you're gifted, you should go to somebody who understands and can guide you, give you guidance, so you can go on to be a healer for the rest of us as life continues on.

Nobody trained me. I see sickness of all kinds. But it's not for me to tell a person, "You've got that kind of sickness in you," unless I am asked by that person. If I'm asked, then I can use my ceremony, and the healing takes place through the songs that come out, not just me talking about it. In other words, you can't train anybody for healing power. We can't train anybody to doctor anybody. It's got to be within their blood. But you can get your healing power from the earth, through herbs, and so on, whatever is out there, to overcome the sickness. You can get help from nature by praying for what's out there.

Visions

There's a vision I've had from way back. Well, I've had visions about a lot of different things, but for instance, not too long ago, something came to me and talked to me about the water here. One time, when we were having a spiritual gathering, when I was praying for the water, the water said to me, "I'm going to look like water, but pretty soon nobody's going to use me." The Creator, or the Spirit told me this, and I passed it on to the people who were there at the time. Now, wherever I go, the people talk about their water being contaminated, and they can't use it.

One particular vision showed me something at the Test Site (U.S. Nuclear Testing Site in southern Nevada)—where they were drilling holes into the earth, and when they blasted those holes, or set those bombs off underground. The vision showed me that place is now beginning to fill up with water. The water is filling up those holes. I saw what it is doing to our earth, inside the earth itself. That's one vision I have seen.

I've seen a lot of visions, but I don't like to talk about them, because generally nobody believes in what I'm saying. It's very hard for people to believe these things. I don't like to talk about most of them. They are things that I don't think anybody would really understand. But there are visions among all of us, not only Indian people; white men also have visions. That's why today the gifted white man goes out there and does his thing—because of the vision he has seen. He wants to follow that vision. For instance, the people coming into Rock Creek canyon, most of the ones I've talked to have had a vision: they've had a vision saying that it's a very important canyon to living human beings. People have to realize that we all have visions, and when we have a vision, we have to follow the vision and see for ourselves if it is true.

Some of us understand what a vision is, even though it's something that everybody has. All the living things on this planet of ours, everything has a vision. Even the planet itself has a vision, and now it's beginning to warn us that something's going to become different pretty quick, if we don't do something about it. This kind of vision is given from the earth to the people, but the people aren't paying attention to the visions. We think they're just something that we've dreamed up, or something that we just don't understand.

Photo: Nancy Clemens

"People have to realize that we all have visions, and when we have a vision, we have to follow the vision and see for ourselves if it is true."

Coming Out from Behind the Bush

As we all know, our water is going to be pretty precious. I think we all realize this today. I talk about this, and I hope people out there will continue to talk about this, and not be behind the bush like I was. I used to be behind the bush with what I know; I never could come out from behind that bush. Now it's time for us all to come out from behind that bush and start hollering. I don't' care how we do it, as long as we do it together.

Actually, the Indian is wise; he understands what's out there, but he doesn't say a thing about it. I notice how my people are. We talk circles around you before we come in with what we really know. In other words, you've got to be really friendly with them before they'll start spilling the beans. I have known this for a long time.

An Indian person might know what is going on with things, but the Indian is the one guy who's not going to come out and say, "Let's do this or that," or "You have to see it this way; this is the way it should be." Indian people are not that type of people. An Indian is always standing behind the bush. They know what's going on, but they don't want to come out and say, "I know this and I know that."

The Indian or Native life is a totally, different, old way of life. Natives don't go out and start saying, "I know what's happening here." They don't usually speak up. They stand behind the bush, like I was until the last few years. I never spoke out before. I never talked to people until lately, and then it was only because I began to see things looking so sad, and because the Spirit came to me and said, "Well, you're going to have to give us a hand, here." How can one person give a hand, unless I bring it all out on the surface?

Taking Care of What We've Got

My belief is to take care of what we've got in order to continue on. The Shoshone—well, not only the Shoshone, but the Native people of all the land, you know, all over the world— believe in taking care of what's now here, in taking care of the world, in other words. Our belief from long ago, for many a moon, has been to take care of what's out there.

In order to get the land green, we have to talk to the Creator. The Creator is the one who puts it here and puts us here to take care of it. So when we take any rocks or anything off the Mother Earth, we have to talk to them and explain why we're taking them from their homes. It's just like we do to build the sweat lodge, when we go out there and get the rocks. I have to tell them the reason why we are removing them from their homes, and where and why they are being taken—for the purpose of having sweat. That's just one example.

Also, all the plant life needs to have somebody talking to it, in order for each plant to continue its life; and in order for us to talk to all the different kinds of plant life, we have to do that through a spirit. A spirit has to talk to us, and it keeps telling us to pray for moisture, for example, to bring moisture to the land. Today a lot of our land is drying up, because we haven't been praying for it. We have to pray for the water. It's a very dangerous situation. If we wipe out these plants, where, how are we going to survive?

Our Indian belief is, we are Natives of the land, and so we have to be with it. But nowadays we haven't been doing what we've been told to do, to be with the land. We have to take care of the living things here, all the plants, all the animal life. When we take the life of an animal, we have to tell it why we're taking its life. It has to know the reason. Then we give the animal a blessing, and then we also give something back of whatever we're taking.

We can't just go out and harvest whatever we want to. We have to talk to each living thing and bless it and say the reason why we're taking its life—the plant, the animal, the bird life, whatever. We have to explain our reasons. They need to know the reasons why we're taking their lives. If they were to take our life, we'd want to understand why they were taking it. These are our strong beliefs.

We've been taught this from the beginning of our lives: *take care of this land and everything that's on it; take care of it well in order to bring good to all the plant life and all the things that are here.* We have to take care of them all. It is very important for us today, as I see it, to come back to the Native way of life. *The Native way is to pray for everything.*

The water has a life, and we have to pray for it. All the water that comes from the Mother Earth, that's her blood. It's the Mother Earth's blood. Just like when water comes out in our tears and rolls down our face, it's the same thing with the water that comes from the mountains, or wherever it comes from; it comes from within the Mother Earth. Then the water gets out there and breaks everything out—all the living things. That's why, as in the sweat, I say that laughing and crying are two good things for us, for all the human race, and even for the animal race, the

Photo: Scott Foglesong

bird life, and everything else. The water is a good thing for all the living things, and it's very important we take care of it.

The rocks are the same way. The rocks talk—they eat like we do; they breathe air like we do. They have the same age as whatever was here thousands of years ago. Some of your people are just beginning to realize that the rocks have a life.

All the plant life has life just like we do. Their spirits are out there. Even the breeze that we breathe; it's got Spirit. It comes around us, and sometimes you can hear things. Sometimes you can hear music from it. As Indian people, those are the things we talk to. Spirit is out there, out there all around us.

This is all very important to the Indian people. We've been told to take care of what we've got in order that we'll be allowed to continue on and in order to leave something for the younger generation for continuing their life. We were supposed to practice these things from the beginning of our lives, but we've forgotten our way—we went on the wrong road, as I like to say. We're off course, and now we're trying to pick up the pieces, but it's very hard to do.

Today I think we, as red people, are coming back to taking care of things. Not only the red people, but today everybody is recognizing the need to take care of what we've got. Everybody, I don't care who they are, what they look like, or what color they are—we're all going to have to start working together to save our planet here.

We've only got one planet to take care of, one planet floating out here in the air. This is the one carrying us, carrying everything out here. We've only got one water that comes from within the Mother Earth.

We've only got one air that we breathe: we all breathe the same air all around this globe. In other words, everything is the same. There's no difference in the air over here and the air over there. There's no difference in the water; there's no difference anywhere for anything on the Mother Earth. The Mother Earth provides us with food, provides us with air, provides us with water. That's why we've only got one air, one water, one Mother Earth that we've got to take care of.

From this, a lot of things follow. I pray in the mornings for the sun, the air, the water, plants, the animals, the rocks. Those prayers have been passed on down from way back for thousands of years, but we haven't been doing enough of these things, of taking care of things, and now we have to come back to it. *We are going to have to start taking care of things again.*

Rules and Regulations

Other humans were here before us. Animals were here before us. But they didn't follow the rules and regulations that were given to them. So now we find them in the sand. We find them in the rocks. Then we say, "They *were* here; they *used* to be here."

That's what they're going to be saying about *us*, if we don't take care of this Earth. They're gonna be saying, "They were here at one time." Somebody else, not us, will be saying this. A different kind of rules and regulations are going to have to be put to us again, because right now we're violating the natural law. We shouldn't be doing that.

These so-called laws that we've got today, they make them every hour on the hour. Then they keep changing the law, because whoever presents it doesn't like the law of whoever presented it before, so they make another law to replace the first one.

There's no such thing as that for red people. The law that the Creator put here is the law that they go by. The leaf of the tree turns different colors at a certain time of the year. That's the law. All the birds recognize it. All the animals recognize it. All the plant life recognizes and lives by those laws.

The water does the same thing. At certain times of the year, the water is colder. At certain times of the year, the water is warmer. But today, in certain places, the water has been hot during the winter months and cold during the summer months, and this is a sign that we're not taking care of the Creator's work, nature's work—that's the law that we cannot change.

Here's something else that the Indian people, my people, used to talk about. Once upon a time, all the trees, the sagebrush, all the bird life, animal life, and all the life, everything, would all get together. There is still a place where I've been, right out of Ely (Nevada), between Ely and Kern Creek—there's a big mound where the animals actually sat in a circle, where they talked about a lot of different things. All those rocks piled up there, those were all the different animal life that became stone. And all the rocks and the birds and the animals, they used to talk; they had voices, and, as I realize it, they've still got a voice today. This is why my people have always said, you have to take care of all those living things in order to be able to continue. If you don't, when they die off, you are going to die with them.

My elders used to tell me that the Indian people are going to have to be strong, because some day the red man is going to have to lead the rest of the people in the right direction. The people who lived here before stopped working with nature, so their life ended on this Mother Earth. The last cycle ended with those huge monsters who lived here a few thousand years ago. They came to an end because they didn't understand what the earth was doing, or how to work with nature. The wind took their life with blowing sand, and today you can find them in sandstone all over the country. Looking at them, I think that's true.

The Indian or Native people, the Shoshone people, never really said too much about anything; they just told stories here and there, what we would call stories today. But as I remember it and understand it, they weren't stories, but history, even though we thought it was a story. As I look at it now, what the Indian people talked about was really true. Just like the Hopi said: we have three roads that we have to follow: the top road, where there is an end to the road; the middle road, where it's going to be mixed with something else; or the third road, the

Photo: Scott Foglesong

bottom road, where we are going to continue on. The Indian people throughout the world say that anything in a circle can continue on. There's no end to a circle. Actually, I think all the Indian people throughout the country have that kind of knowledge about life.

Today, we really don't know anything about the old ways in which people understood life. Most of my own people don't even know. The older people know, but they won't talk about it because we were always told, "You guys are savages; you don't know anything."

Today these "savages" are beginning to come out and talk about how we are going to have to take care of our Mother Earth.

And there is a way that we can take care of all of this, but it's not for me to say. I have to be told by somebody else, something out there, Spirit, to bring this out. I can't just say it.

However, we already know how we're going to do it. The first step we're going to take is to unite ourselves together. That's the very first step. The second step is, we have to talk to what's out there, to the Creator, the Spirit of all the living things. The third step is the easy one. We have to do what It says, and it's not for me to say how.

We Must Return to the Native Ways

We have to come back to the Native way of life. The Native way is to pray for everything, to take care of everything. We can see what's taking place: the animal life has begun to show us, the tree life is showing us, and the water is even telling us, but we're not paying attention to it.

People today don't realize that what's out there—all the things growing on the land—needs to have our prayers. These things are here on the earth with us. We're part of their life too, and together this is how we are to survive over the long term. All the food plants out in my part of the country have been disappearing because the people don't understand this.

The water, the air, the land are contaminated, and it's not our fault, but still it is our people who were asked to take care of those things. But what are we doing as red people? We're not doing *anything*. We're beginning to get together now, but it's the white man who's telling us, "Hey, you guys are going to have to do something. You are the ones who are going to have to lead us in the right direction, in the ways you took care of the land and everything before. When we came here, the land was beautiful. Then people took advantage of it, and now we have major problems."

For six hundred years, what did the white man do for us? What did they do for Mother Earth? All they did was try and destroy it, and today that's the road we're on.

Now, I don't think we're going to be able to change until we can get our spiritual people together, and in some places the spiritual people have started talking to one another.

Like I say, we have to come back to the natural way of life in order for us to survive. We are going to have to survive off the Mother Earth like our forefathers did for thousands of years. They took care, they prayed for the water, they prayed for the air, they prayed for the same things that I pray for each morning.

Now we *are* beginning to get together. All over the country, the Indian people are saying, "Hey, let's do something." We're beginning to see things differently. Now the truth is coming out about the Indian way of life, and the importance of taking care of what we've got.

As I go around, I see that we are touching a lot of people's hearts. The people of the world have begun to realize that the Native people are bringing things back to the natural way of life.

So I'm asking people to pray. Anybody who wants to pray, pray in your own way, or however you want to pray, even if you say only one word or two. The Indian way, we form a circle and come to the fire, take some ashes, and put them on our forehead; this is what our forefathers used to do. When we put these ashes into our prayer together, they become pretty powerful

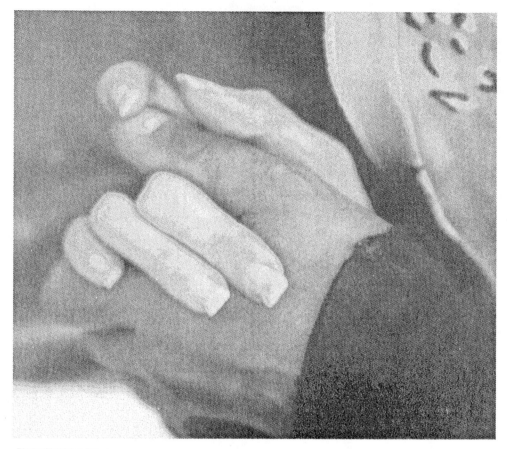

Photo: Hawkeye Haven

ashes. When you pray—I don't care how you do it—always ask for this Mother Earth of ours to continue on, and that the water should be clear and clean when it comes out of the ground.

Prayer is a very important way of uniting people, and we must unite ourselves as one people. If we all pray alike throughout the world, we will have a beautiful world, and we will have peace.

The Truth

Anything written down on a piece of paper is worthless to me. You can keep changing those words and changing them. If you keep changing the words, where's the truth to it? That's my question.

Indian prayers are the same thing over and over again, like a broken record that never wears out, the same thing all the time. Only the Creator itself or Nature itself has the power to change what is said in the prayers, because only they know what the truth is.

People recognize this. As I travel around, people listen to me talk and they say, "He's standing there and he's talking; he's pure, and he's talking about the truth." And some white men that I've talked to in the churches say, "You're pure—you talk about the truth, and it's coming from within you. You might not talk good English, but we understand what you're saying."

I can see by this that people's minds are already being turned towards the Indian people. So we, the Indian people, are going to have to take care of ourselves and start bringing out the natural ways, the truth, for everyone, because no one is going to bring them out for us.

The truth is: take care of what you've got. The air, the water, we all use these alike. The air is saying to us, to me, "I'm here; everybody gets to use me, but take care of me." Water is saying, "If you take care of me, you are going to have clean water. If you don't take care of me, you aren't going to have anything."

The important thing is that when people go outside and see and hear these things for themselves, then they know it's true. They know it's not a lie, because they see it too: the natural

Corbin in Puerto Rico, 1994

beauty *and* the contamination. Looking at the grass, where it's all dried up on the mountainside, or whatever, we can all see what's happening, not only the young people, but also the grown-ups, everybody. So what I'm saying is the truth.

One Water, One Air, One Earth

"The old people used to say that the trees, the rocks, the birds, and the animals used to talk. They had a voice, and today, as I realize it, they still have a voice. My people always say that you have to take care of them in order for you to continue on. If you don't, when they die off, you are going to die off with them." —Corbin Harney

Contamination

As I see it all around me, the trees are dying out, our water is contaminated, and our air is not good to breathe. I always say we took the wrong road, because we thought it was easier, and it is. All we do today is just push a button to do this, push a button to do that. Our forefathers had to do it the way of the Creator who put us here—to take care of everything and to talk to all the living things out there—and we haven't been doing that.

Now look how sad it is. Look at the rain. Now the rain has begun to have a lot of acid in it. When is this acid ever going to be out of whatever's coming down on us? If it doesn't get out of the rain, then where are we going to be? How are we going to clean it up? This question is very important to all of us, to all living things.

In some places where I've been, we're already beginning to suffer. People have been told, don't drink milk, because the milk is contaminated with something. And then there are potatoes.

Photo: Scott Foglesong

In some places, they've already been told not to market their potatoes. The contamination has reached the potatoes. This contamination that we're putting onto the Mother Earth is not the way. I've been down at the Nevada Test Site protesting this for many years.

We're going to have to turn this thing around, somehow, some way, because right now we're in the age of losing our water. Soon, we're not going to be able to drink the water. In some places this has already begun to happen, where the water is mixed with some chemicals. We're not going to be able to survive those chemicals. We know there's contamination on the land today. We know it's in the water, and that it's spreading throughout the world.

We're trying to do something about all this by stopping nuclear development. We're trying to put a stop to this thing that we don't understand but which creates enormous problems for us. I don't know whether we can stop nuclear testing or not, but I know we have all begun to suffer from it. We're all going to have some kind of disease. We are already beginning to see that happening, and it's very dangerous. We have to realize that we are going to have to work with nature if we are going to continue to have life. If we don't, then we're not going to have a life. There will just be nothing, no life at all.

I think that people throughout the country are beginning to say the same things that I am saying: Let's do something about it. Let's unite ourselves together and try to put a stop to this thing that we don't understand. I don't think anybody really understands radioactivity at all, but we're spreading radioactive, nuclear substances all over the country and throughout the air. We're sending nuclear-powered airships towards the moon, the stars, and so forth. What's all that going to do to the air above us? What's it going to do to the ozone layer, the atmosphere around the earth? We've already heard about the ozone layer, with too much of the sun's radioactivity coming towards us today. We're going to have all kinds of sickness. And then, even though we're experiencing all this, we still continue on in the same direction, even when we don't understand the effects of spreading radioactivity.

We have all kinds of bad things today, in the air, in the water, in the soil, and so on which we can never seem to get away from. I don't know whether it's too late right now to clean it up, or whether we can clean it up in time. We can ask nature itself to clean it up, so we'll have a better life in the end. I don't know what it's going to be like within a very short time.

Our One Water

Water is going to be very important. All living things, including the white man, are going to be suffering along with us. We as redskin people, we've got a chance to survive, but only because we're connected to what's out there; we can talk to things. We can ask the water to continue to flow and be cleaner and purer water for us. The Creator listens to us if we talk to Him. Today, in some places, I see that water is getting pretty scarce, and it's getting worse. It's getting contaminated with something.

I'm beginning to see what was told to me when the water said, "I'm going to look like water, but pretty soon nobody's going to use me." In some places the water's already got chemicals in it, so much that they can't use it. And people are just continuing to put poison in that water.

When I went to the coast, the ocean water there looked sad to me. The water is saying, "I need help." Water talks like we do. It breathes air like we do. It's hard to believe, but it does. Everything drinks water, and everything's got a life to it.

The Sacramento River is another place that's contaminated with something so bad that I don't think any fish will live in it again for a long time (referring to a toxic spill on the upper Sacramento, 1989). They are trying to search for something to clean it up, but what, we don't know. Today we have to ask how we are going to be able to save the fish, the ones that still survive in that water, because the life in that water is gone. How are we going to bring the life back into the water?

Even the water in Rock Creek Canyon (Nevada), our spiritual ground, is in sad shape, and it's the same thing with snow. All our rocks used to be pure white only a few years ago, but today they are all greenish.

Photo: Paul Clemens

Rock Creek Canyon

There are four counties right now in California where the water is so contaminated that they can't use it. Even when you boil it, they've been told, you can't get rid of that stuff at all; their water is contaminated so bad that they cannot use it. So now the county commissioners are asking the people to move out and sell their properties. But who are they going to sell them to? They don't know.

Also, in Nevada there are four towns where the water is so bad that the people have already been told that they cannot use their water; they have to haul it in from somewhere else. How long can we haul water from somewhere else? Pretty soon, if everything is contaminated with something else, where are we going to be? The next generations after us, the young, the unborn—how are they going to survive?

We're already seeing things drying up that shouldn't be drying up. And we have already been told that our milk is beginning to be contaminated with radioactivity, by radioactive dumping on our land and by cows eating that grass.

What are they doing today throughout the country so that the water is not pure anymore? Most everywhere throughout my travels, I see people carrying jugs of water that come from Safeway. When Safeway runs out of water, where are we going to go then? Where will we get our water?

We are suffering for water, for pure water, not only in this part of the country, but also abroad, all around the globe. When I was in Sweden, where they've got plenty of water, lots of lakes and so forth, I was told by their people when I went out there and looked at it, that the water is not pure. It's kind of greenish in color, between blue and green, and they said that the water is not good now. So today, here and now, it's very important that we join hands together, because we've only got one Earth, and we've only got one Water. We share a life, and we have to take care of it.

There are a lot of things going on, like at the Nevada Test Site— when they set off a bomb a thousand feet within the Mother Earth—what does it do to our water table? Our water table is getting mixed up with all this uranium and radioactive stuff that they are blasting down there, and our government doesn't tell us the truth about it, and they try to keep us distracted by telling us it's not dangerous, it's just a test, it won't harm us. But then our people are dying throughout the country by the thousands.

When I was over in Kazakhstan, I found out that many people over there are dying, but the government doesn't tell us about

Photo: Scott Foglesong

those things. In Utah, a lot of people have died and are still dying today on account of the uranium. This nuclear power—we talk about how powerful it is. We have to get together to overcome this and say NO to that uranium. We should leave it alone.

As the Indian people said a long time ago, "If you don't take care of what you have now, you're not going to have anything." I've been told that lots of times, and now it's coming true. They told me, some day you're going to wake up and not have a thing. That's just about where we're at today.

People have a hard time believing all this because the people don't believe in each other. They don't have any way to believe in their own selves, because they've lied to each other so badly that everything's in a scramble. So today nobody believes anybody else, because that's the way life supposedly is: you can't believe anything until you see it for yourself. It's been that way since the Wolf and the Coyote first talked over the rules and the regulations.

You see, the coyote and the wolf were talking long ago. The wolf was arguing that we should all look alike: the rocks should be the same, the sagebrush the same, all the humans the same, and all the living things on this planet should be the same. We should think alike and act alike and so forth.

But the coyote always said, "No, we should all be different. We shouldn't look alike at all."

And so, today, we look around us and nothing looks alike. Rocks are not alike. Humans are not alike. This is the root of why we don't believe in each other. It's just as the coyote said: There's no use believing in just one thing. Let's not believe it. Let's all disagree, and everybody believe in different things. That's why I always say, it's easy to believe the bad things first, but the good thing is harder to believe, and harder to come by. As the wolf said, "It's going to be really hard that way, because what you're saying is, let's not believe in each other."

So today, what the coyote said is what we've got, and I've witnessed it so far. It's very dangerous that we don't believe in each other, but there's no way that we can ever believe in each other, because the rules and regulations were set by the people who were here before us as animals. They became animals while they were humans. And today, the coyote is the same as he was a million years ago, and we're living according to what he said: we don't believe in each other, and we always disagree. We

"Today, water is very important. We redskin people have a chance to survive because we're connected to what's out there. We can talk to a lot of things. We can ask the water to continue to flow and be purer and cleaner water for us. The Creator listens to us if we talk to him."

Photo: Scott Foglesong

disagree with whatever it is out there that we hear about. We don't believe it unless we see it, and even then we only believe part of it, not all of it. History and everything else shows us that. But, like I say, we do have to believe in somebody, someday. We will have to experience for ourselves, what we can do, what we can say to each other, and so on. We are really going to have to work at this, because the time is getting shorter and shorter.

Today everything is warning us about the bad things that are coming, and that we shouldn't be disagreeing with each other. We should look at those things and say, "Let's do something about them."

All the people I've talked to so far say, "Can you prove it? Can you prove this is so and so?" They don't believe it unless they see it, and then they still don't believe it. They figure the proof was put there by somebody just to make you believe it. But it's not so. As I see it, we're not going to believe in these dangers until they happen. And then it'll be too late. Then who are we going to tell it to in the next go around?

A few years ago the water said to me, when I was praying for the water, "I'm going to look like water, but pretty soon nobody's going to use me." Those words came from the water, the Spirit. And the next morning I asked the same question again: "Why did you say that? What was the reason?"

And now I'm realizing the truth of what the water said, because even in the ocean, where there's such a huge amount of water—you look across that water and you never see the end, and I never realized how big a water it was—but that water today is contaminated with uranium and all kinds of things. The fish are already dead in the big ocean, but we don't fully understand why they're dying. I've seen about seven sea lions dead on the shoreline. Why are they dying on the shorelines? Their kind are supposed to go into the middle of the ocean to die, so that something else can survive on them. Those are the things that we Native people watch. When huge animals come on shore to die, we know that's not their way.

I've been saying this for a long time, that our water is becoming contaminated. We're not going to have fresh water.

So, now, we're there. We're there. I don't care how we look at it or what we say in different parts of the country or different states and so forth. We're not going to have clean water very long, because the contamination is already here among us, in California and in other places, where they say you had better buy your water. Okay, but then, are they guaranteeing this water that we are supposed to buy? It's coming from Safeway or Albertsons or wherever. Are we all going to be carrying around those bottles? What about our animal friends? What about our bird friends? How are they going to carry theirs? Where are they going to get theirs? Down the line pretty quick, where are we going to get ours? That's where we're headed right now.

The Water at Rock Creek Canyon

The water here looks pretty clean, when it comes from the mountains. It comes a short ways, but it's still not as clean as it used to be ten years ago. This water is very important to all the living things on this Mother Earth. If we can keep it clean, then we will have clean water to drink, clean water to bathe with.

All living things like to enjoy clean water. The rocks right here, they want clean water. The tree life has to have clean water. We are all one life, and clean water is something we have to rely on.

Life began with clean water. Life began with everything clean; the same with the air. The water has to have air; it has to have clean air in order to make all this racket going down the canyon here. We have to revere water as a living thing. We're all alive out here. Our Spirit is out here, and the Spirit has to have clean water.

Photo: Paul Clemens

The water here has begun to turn green. So that means there are chemicals up there behind us. The high mountains catch all the bad air—and that's why we have to pray for the water, the air, the mountains, and everything all together.

In order to have clean water, we have to continue asking for cleaner water than it is today. As I stand over the water here and look at it as it goes over the white rocks, I see green things beginning to accumulate. That's poison—it's something I don't think anything can live with—and today, sure enough, there are very few fish in here that survive. There aren't too many alive in this water, because they're not getting the cleaner water that they're used to.

We have to take care of this. All of us have to work together to have cleaner water. This is why the Indian people always say, "Everything has to be clean as we go down the road." The water is very important to us. I see it here. It's making noise. It's talking to us. It's singing a song to us. The water's song is very important.

The water has been saying to us, just as it is now, "Please pray for me, so I can have a cleaner life." I think we hear that coming from the water's voice: "Keep me clean, so I can have a cleaner life," the water says right here, "because I like to be clean. I don't like being contaminated with something." That's what the water is saying all over the country, but you can hear it real clearly right here. I can hear it. I don't know whether other people can hear it or not, but it's saying that to me. "Keep me clean, clean."

The water's not clean. Why else would it be saying, "Keep me clean," if it's not clean? So, there must be something in it right now. Like I say, the rocks have begun to turn green here. You can see it for yourself. Right here, these used to be white rocks, and within a short time, they've turned green. So the water is getting poisoned somewhere, which it doesn't want. I think that's why the water is saying, "Keep me clean—I'd like to have a cleaner life."

You see, this water has a Spirit. It's got a life like we do, the same thing. That's why it's saying these things, saying how very important it is that we keep it clean, so all living things can have clean water. I can hear what it's saying. I've talked about what the Creator tells me, but here I can actually hear the voice coming from the water itself, saying those things. But I tell you, the water's not going to continue saying these things. Once we kill the life that's in it, it won't have a voice like we have any longer. It won't have the strength.

Today the water doesn't have the same strength it used to have even ten years ago. This water right here is very important to me, but all over the world today, we don't have clean water.

In some places the water is already so that you can't use it, especially in mining towns. We already know that; most people have seen it on TV, so I don't have to tell people about it, but I keep repeating it over and over again because I'd like to see us work together as much as possible to clean our world and have a beautiful world to live in. To do that, everything has to take care of that water.

The water has said to us before, "You take care of me; I'll cleanse you. I give you myself, and you can have a clean life. But if you don't take care of me, then I'll dry up, and then you won't have anything." The water has said to me, "I'm going to look like water, but some day nothing's going to use me." And now I see that coming about.

The meaning of what the water said, as I see it, is that it is going to be contaminated with something that is very dangerous. It means we have to put a stop to this nuclear testing, because it's going to contaminate our water, contaminate our air. Everything is going to become contaminated with something. When I was down at the coast, I saw how we're spilling chemicals into the ocean water, spilling gas, oil, and all kinds of garbage into it. This is a very dangerous thing, just as the water said to me. I already see that what the water said is coming about. I think we all understand that vision. We all understand what this is about.

If we ignore these warnings, we are going to be a people who are not here any more. It's a warning given to us. What it's going to be like after that, nobody knows. There will be no life, I think. No earth, nothing. If we are going to have a life, it's going to be on a different kind of planet, I think. It won't be this one, because this one here is going to be gone. If we don't have our water or our air, nothing is going to grow here.

Prayers and Ceremony

The Native Way Is to Pray

This is the Native way: all of us are related to everything else, to the elements, to all the animal life. We're all connected to the tree life, too—you name it. We're all the same. We're all a part of the water, too—some of us don't realize it, but we are. We are part of the air, and we are part of the fire.

We're part of everything here on Earth, and we're part of the moon, sun, and stars. We're all connected together here. Indian people always pray to all those things so that they keep moving in the right direction, so that they'll keep us nice and clean, and so we can have a healthier life. That's what we are saying to all those things in our prayers.

The Native way is to pray for everything.

As a native of this land, I talk in my native tongue. When I talk about the fire, the rocks, the sunrise, the air, and the water, I pray for those things, pray to make them clear. The water, when we drink water, I'm asking the water to come out of the Mother

Photo: Hawkeye Haven

Earth clear and pure. That way all the living things, all the plant life, and everything else can live on healthy. I'm asking the same thing of the wind, that the wind help clean the air for us to breathe, clean the air for all the living things on this Mother Earth, all the birds, animals, all those lives that we really have to depend on.

The government made a treaty with the Shoshone people, yet never kept up their end of the bargain at all. We, as an Indian people, we did try to follow the treaty all the way. We put our weapons away, told them, by God, we're not going to fight with you. You can go ahead and use our land, use our water. We used whatever we got out there all together, but they wanted it all for themselves.

Right now again today, they say they're going to take away our water and everybody's fighting for water permits and so on. How does the Creator look at all this? I think this water was put here on this Mother Earth for all of us to use, all the living things out here, not only the human race, but everybody was supposed to use it . . . all the birds, plant life, tree life, animal life and so on. For some reason, we're not considering them. We're only think-ing about ourselves.

We can see what's taking place. I think everybody already knows. The animal life began to show us, the bird life is showing us, the tree life is showing us, even the water is telling us, but we're not paying attention to it. But I think we are going to start paying attention to this pretty quick. Everybody is talking about acid rain, for one. It's going to cover the whole world if we don't do something about it now.

The Native people always think of the earth first, because we've been told to take care of what we've got.

Where Our Power Comes From

It's very important that we be connected to the elements as a human race. As a Native person, I am connected to these things, because I can hear their voices, coming from all these elements. I hear all their songs and everything else. I'm asking each thing to continue on in a good way, and doing this is very important to me, because this is where my power comes from. I have to *do* something so that all this continues on.

In order to connect with all these things, our forefathers had to have ceremony and pray. That was our duty. I have to use my eagle feathers in my ceremony because I'm connected to them. Those eagle feathers are telling me things; I can vision things using them. It's very important for me to be able to use my eagle feathers and to keep having my visions. Once I quit, I don't know who's going to take over these things, because we've all been getting away from our connections to the earth. We've been going the wrong direction; I keep saying that to people. We're supposed to be taking care of the land, taking care of the earth, but we haven't been doing our job. The white man began by telling us that we were doing things wrong, but we weren't and we're not.

I think everyone is now coming back to realize that the Indian people have the authority to talk about the right way to care for the earth. We've always spoken the truth about this, about how we're connected to the earth, about what the animals are doing, what the birds are doing, what the waters are doing, and so forth. And now, today, we all know that everything is made connected to what's out there.

Prayer to Water

These are my prayers to water in the mornings. I try to do the best I can with what little gift I've got, to try and connect with what's out there, to try to keep the water clean, as much as I have the power to do. To pray, I talk about our water:

Clean us, when we drink you.
Be good to us, so we'll have a healthier body.

Make sure you take care of what's out here, all the trees, all
the living things that are on this Mother Earth, all the
plant life, the birds, and so forth.
Continue to flow clean, so that we have clean water to
drink.

To the water that comes out of the ground, I'm saying:

Be pure and clean, so that when we use you, you keep us
healthy, and so you can continue to be clean for us and
all the living things.
Make sure that when you come from within the earth, make
sure you're clean.
When we use you, when we drink you, make sure you give us
strength and energy, and when we take a bath with you,
I'm asking you, Water, to continue to give us a good
feeling, with whatever we do with you, in whatever way
we use you, so that all the living things, all the plant life,
everything that uses you in any way, that everything can
be clean.

This is some of what I say to the water.

I pray every morning for everything, for the water, for the
land. For everything, I ask for good things.

I pray to the Earth to continue to rotate in a clean way.

I talk to rocks in my prayers. I ask the rocks,

Make sure that you are in such a way that we hear from you.

Make your voices heard; make sure that I hear what you're
   saying.
Make sure that when we walk on you, we don't stumble on you.
Rocks, I'm asking you to continue to be good to us in all
   ways, and not to harm us.

That's what I say to the rocks.

Sometimes I talk for a few hours to all our plant life. I tell our
food to continue to grow. All our food life must have a good life,
too.

I pray that you continue to have a good life.
I pray that you have good soil to stand on, and that every-
   thing that gives us food is good, and that you go about
   living your lives just as we do.
I pray that you continue to grow, and have good roots, so that
   we can feed on you in order to stay healthy, and that the
   food you make gives us the strength we need.

I ask the fire to burn clean, to cook our food in such a way
that it won't harm us.

Fire, burn clean.
Burn clean so that we can use you.
You can warm the Mother Earth when you burn, but don't
   harm anything.
Make sure that we, as the people, and the animal life, and the
   bird life, can use you to heat our bodies, so that way we
   keep our Mother Earth as clean as can be.

Fire, keep on burning.

When I pray to the fire, I also pray to smoke and to the ashes. The smoke talks to us, just like all the other things do. And we all use ashes, even though some of us don't realize that we do. You can get them in the drugstores, where you go to get pills. My people, the Native people, use ashes to put into their food, into their soup, their coffee, whatever. In order to have a clean stomach, you have to have ashes in your system. The Native people have used ashes for thousands of years. Wherever there's a fire, the animals go around licking the ashes. So we have to take care of our fire. It's something that warms us, warms our body, and cooks our food for us.

Prayer to Ashes

Like I say, ashes are something that we all should carry. My forefathers have used ashes for thousands of years. They put ashes on themselves in order to feel healthy as they walked the Earth, to walk clean and have a good feeling as they walked the Earth. So the ashes that we pray to are a very important part of our life.

We all use ashes, but we don't realize it. The white man isn't using ashes today that I know of. Ashes are what cooks our food, warms our body, and keeps us alive at night. But nowadays we push buttons and whatnot. Long ago this was the only light we had. This "still flame," as we call it, keeps the spirit alive. So the ashes are very important; we say our prayer to ashes when we pray to the fire.

When I pick up the ashes, the spirit might tell me I have to spread them on all the people, so they can be a part of those ashes, so that's where our prayer comes in. The ashes have the power for us to be healthier and to continue to live.

The way I do it is, through the ashes in my hand, I pray for the ashes and then spread them about. In some places they put the ashes in their food, to have ashes in their bodies.

Offering Tobacco

We bless and pray for the smoke. We offer tobacco—Indian tobacco, not this fancy tobacco nowadays—to bless whatever we are going to get. Today we're all packing smoke as an offering.

Tobacco is an offering to the fire, and to each other. That's what the tobacco is all about, because if the land here burns by man-made causes, it will never come back again. If the fire is started by nature, all of what's out here will come back, even better than it was. The Indian people say that it's really good when that happens, that then the land will come back greener, which is true. But a man-made cause is altogether different.

I'm proud when I notice people offering something to something. It's very important. It's the reason that Indian people live to be a hundred years or over: they work together, they bless one another, and they always give tobacco to each other.

The smoke heals us. The smoke said one time, thousands of years ago, "I'll cover the world, and when I purify myself, I'll clear the earth, the air, the water, and so forth. We have witnessed that at times. Look at Yellowstone Park a few years ago.

The fire covered it, and the smoke said, "When I clear myself, everything's going to turn green," which is true.

Sagebrush

Sagebrush at one time said, "I don't care how wet I am; when you ask me to warm your body, I'll burn." You can float it in the ocean water, but still it will burn for you, to give you a healing, in other words. This is what the sage said.

We've all used sage at one time or another. Our forefathers, when they first came to this country, used sage to heal their sick. Today we're still doing it, the same as we have done for thousands and thousands of years. This is what keeps the air clean and so on, along with the trees which continue to purify our air.

Prayers to Sun and Wind

I pray to the sun to continue to shine, just as my forefathers have done for thousands of years. I continue to practice the same thing.

Sun, continue to shine on us, to shine on the Mother Earth
here, and make a good reflection on us, so that you will
shine in a way that warms the Mother Earth.
Continue to shine on Mother Earth, on all the animals, the
birds, the fish, and the human race, on all the flowers,
and on all our food, so that they all continue to grow.

I pray for the sun and the wind.

Wind, continue to have a breeze,
    so that we have clean air to breathe.
Continue to move everything,
    move everything here on the Mother Earth,
    so that you continue to give us fresh air.

And Sun, if there is a problem, a bad thing,
    make the breeze to blow that away from us,
    so that way we can have cleaner air.

Prayer for Rain

We have to get together like our forefathers did to bring moisture of some kind wherever the land is parched.

I ask for moisture to fall upon us
    so the grass will start to grow.
I pray for moisture for the things that survive on the grass,
    what we humans tromp down.
The food that all the creatures are supposed to eat,
    we tramp it down so it's flat on the ground.
So we know it's up to us; together we have to ask for the rain
    to come down, so the grass will continue to grow again.

Everything in the land relies upon us. If we're all in one place together, we pray for all the things in that place. Don't forget any of this. This is the way life goes. We have to pray for each other, to take care of each other. We have to take care of what's out there. We have to take care of what we've got. Now I feel raindrops on my head; I don't know why.

Prayer to Mountain

I bless the mountain by asking the mountain to bless us:

Mountain, because you're here, sticking out of the ground,
it's very important that you take care of our water
when it comes from you, from underneath you.
Make sure the water comes out clean from you—
so we can use you, pure, clean Water,
and so we can drink you and wash with you.

And now I ask you, today, Mountain,
to continue to have a voice,
to have songs—because through you,
we can hear the wind whistle through your rocks.
And your jagged rocks, I'm asking you rocks to be sure
to take care of my bird, the Eagle, so that he may land
and fly over you in a healthier way,
and so he'll feel good flying on top of you.

Photo: Hawkeye Haven

This is what I say to the mountain. It's a very short version of my prayers, just as an example. If the mountain doesn't have a voice, then we as a people are not going to have a voice pretty quick. All the living things are not going to have any voice, because the mountain is where the voice comes from.

The mountain is where the people are, the little people up there, the mountain people, as we call them, or the rock people—they're up there listening to us. They're the ones we have to pray to; they're the ones who take care of the mountain. If we don't ask them, then we're leaving them out, and we can't leave them out. They're the ones who take care of the water when it flows from the mountains, who make sure it's clean when it comes from the mountain. Some people may not believe these mountain people exist, but I have seen them.

They're visible if you have the gift to see them. So they're really there.

If we don't take care of all these things, like I always say, then we're not going to have anything clean. We have to ask what's out there, the rocks, the land, the living things, to unite together; everything has to work together.

Long ago, the land, the mountain, used to have more voice, a clearer voice, clearer than what it is today. The land, the rocks, they used to continue to tell us over and over again to take care of them and to ask us to do those things.

But today, we're lost, and I think it's the reason we're not concerned with anything; we just look at a mountain as if it's just there, nothing more. But the mountain's got a life to it. Everything's got a spirit, the mountain's got a spirit, and all the living things on the mountain have got a spirit.

You'll see an eagle fly over the top of a mountain. The eagle stays up high because it's cleaner there. They like to have clean air. However, as time goes on, we're not going to have clean air; after a while, we're not going to have anything for them to eat.

Nowadays we see animal life beginning to come down to the lower elevation, even though they should be up higher where it's cool. It's one of the reasons why their voice is not clear and loud anymore—because we haven't been taking care of them.

Prayer at Sunrise

When my people pray at sunrise, they talk to the sun. They stand still, looking at the sunrise when it peeks over the horizon. The bird does the same thing. You notice that all the birds will sit facing that direction for a few seconds, and then they'll

Photo: Hawkeye Haven

"I pray for the sun to continue to shine on us,
like my forefathers have done for thousands of years.
I pray for the sun to continue to shine on the Mother Earth,
on the animals, the birds, the human race, the fish, on the flowers,
and all our food, so that everything continues to grow."

continue on with what they were doing. At the same time, that's when the grass, you name it, begins to move and starts opening up.

Most people have flowers around their yard. If you look at them in the morning, they'll be sleeping. They'll start to open when the sun rises. The birds start to sing a little before sunrise. When it's still kind of dark yet, the birds will make a lot of racket, but right at sunrise, everything will quiet and just stand still. You don't hear them for a few seconds—and then the sun peeks over the horizon, and then they'll start up again.

Sun, rise up on us, so that all living things here on Earth can rise up with you.

The Native people have sung a sunrise song for thousands of years. This song is very important to the Native people, to the land, the air that we breathe, and to the Mother Earth. The song is for the purpose of taking care of what we've got and for having Mother Earth in good health, so that we can continue to survive here on the Earth.

It's an important song for the Creator, Spirit, and all that are here. Those spirits are here among us. The spirits have to hear those songs in order to feel better that we are here along with them, but they are here whether or not we sing.

All living things are happy to see us when we are all here together. All this is not for show. It's something that we were born into, and it's something that we must live by. It is simply the rules and regulations that the Indian people have to follow. The rules aren't tough, but they're good. We feel better, feel good together, when we have songs and make our prayers. Everyone feels good when we pray together to the Creator, or whatever; it makes your heart feel lighter.

I speak in my native tongue in the morning ceremony, and this is very important to me, because this borrowed tongue is very hard for me to understand. And while I pray, I always ask whoever is there to turn around to the sun and to bless themselves, to go ahead and bless themselves, because the sun is important to all of us.

I pray this morning, Sun, that as you come out,
  you will warm our bodies and cause all living things
  to grow on this Earth; for without you
  coming out every day, Sun, nothing will survive.

I pray that you will keep us healthy, keep us pure.

I pray that the air will remain pure and help our bodies
  keep in wellness.
Keep this great spirit among us.

I pray that all living things on this earth will continue to live,
  and that all creatures that fly over the earth
  will fly feeling good and continue living among us
  and with us.

I ask you to come out clear, to warm this Mother Earth,
  so that we can appreciate your light
  and what it does for us.

All the plant life depends on you.
They feel healthier when you come up clear on top of them.
All the plant life here depends on you.
We are all welcoming you, coming over the horizon.

Photo: Scott Foglesong

"All living things are happy to see us
when we are all here together. . . .
Every one feels good when we pray together
to the Creator."

We also pray to the moon in the morning ceremony. We talk about how the moon sits and what it does. And we also pray for all the stars, the morning stars, as we call them, and sometimes we talk to the evening stars.

We are living things that grow as the sun comes out. The sun reminds us every day that we should pray to the Great Spirit, to all the living things that surround the Earth, and that we should continue to pray that the air will remain pure, that the springs, the water, will keep running, and keep everything green, and wash our bodies, and keep our throats from going dry.

Morning Circle

When we form a circle for the morning ceremony, I ask people to stand straight up and down, standing up on Mother Earth. We make as perfect a circle as we can. The circle is important, because ceremony ties in with the fire. Fire ties in with the land.

I use some cedar, some herbs that I get off my own land in that part of the world. And when I gather them, I pray for them, I bless them, and I have to give something when I take it out of the ground. None of us can just go over there and grab something and take it out of the ground. We have to talk to it first.

There's a song for everything. There's a song for the cedar. The fire has a song. The smoke has its song, you name it.

Prayer with Cedar

Here's the reason I pray with cedar. At one time we all used cedar. I don't care what kind of ceremony we had, all over the world, we used cedar. Cedar at one time said to us, "When you put me over a rock, the fire, or whatever, or when you breathe

Photo: Paul John Miller/Black Star

me, I'll cleanse you from the inside, because I've got a clean root. I'm the one that gives the good smell to whatever is out here. I was here before you, and I'll continue to grow alongside you."

Now everybody carries cedar with them. Wherever you go, you see a lot of people carrying little pouches with cedar in them. I even saw that over there in Stockholm, some people carrying little tiny pouches of cedar. Cedar is something that continues to grow right alongside of us. Cedar was here before we became human beings.

We have to use cedar, to cleanse ourselves, smoke ourselves, and smoke our homes.

I ask you, Cedar, to smoke, to give us here
   all that clean smell inside us, to cleanse us, purify us,
   purify our thinking, purify our homes.

Pine Nut Song

The pine nut song is very short. It doesn't have too many words to it. It sings about the pine nuts that are scattered over the lands. In other words, the pine nuts are not together. That song is part of my morning ceremony because the pine nuts put that song to me:

Puhuwah—scattered—I'm scattered; no one is praying to me.

That is what the pine nuts said at one time, and the reason the song is that way is that the pine nut tree is scattered throughout. Pine nuts are getting pretty scarce. They've almost all been cut down. We have to look throughout the land to find any; they're not together anymore.

Standing Up

When I pray, everyone has to stand up straight, because the tree stands up straight and all the animals stand up straight. Even the grass stands up. We, as a red people, always say we have to stand up to pray, and I have to do so.

My people stand up to pray, with the soles of their feet right next to the Earth. And they had to take off their shoes; that is,

*"The Native people always think of the earth first,
because we've been told to take care of what we've got."*

"*All the living things
here have to be prayed to
because they're alive like
we are. Everything's got a
life and a spirit to it, and
we have to take care of it
and pray for it so it will
live on for the younger
generation.*"

Photo: Hawkeye Haven

they wore moccasins. That was hard work for them, especially for women folks. The women had a legging that went half way up their leg. The men folks didn't. They had to take off their moccasins every morning prayer, because they had to have their feet right next to Mother Earth. When you are praying, you can feel that energy coming right through the bottom of your feet. When you're asking the Creator to help us, and give us an energy, you can feel it come through your legs. That's why they had to take off their shoes, or whatever they had on.

All living things stand up, upwards. You don't see anything upside down. All the plant life stands up from the Earth. Everything is that way.

Look at the mountains. They're not upside down; the mountains go upwards. This is very important. Today the white man has it in his books, what I'm talking about, what I have prayed to. Thirty or forty years ago, he didn't have those things, but now it's showing up in the white man's books that the tree is standing straight up, that all your energy comes up from the bottom of your feet. So what I'm saying is the truth, what I have seen in my time.

When I ask people to stand up and pray, many people tell me that they've never heard that before, that this is the first time, and that it was really nice to hear those things coming from a Native person.

For several years I've been talking to people about standing up, about how the energy comes from the bottom of your feet. After I talked about that, I heard that a guy from Las Vegas stood up there and repeated the same thing that I'm saying—that everything stands up straight from the Earth—but even though he was saying it, he didn't realize that this is where all the energy comes from.

In the Sweat Lodge

This is a sacred thing. The white people don't totally understand the sweat lodge. They don't understand the way we pray,
the way we take care of things, the way we take care of each
other, and so on. That's why I've invited them to the Test Site
and to help us preserve our sacred burial sites and sacred
grounds. I've said for the past few years, "Bring everybody in, get
the camera out there, and take pictures, so we can spread what's
happening out around the world." This is the only way we're
going to get recognized, and the only way everybody's going to
start saying, "Hey, we're going to have to work together to save
our Earth here." And that's the bottom-line aim of the whole
thing. So we've been bringing white people into the sweat to
teach them the true understanding.

The sweat lodge is sacred for several reasons. We don't do it
just to go in there and sit down and sing songs and pray. There
are a lot of different ways to use it. For the people of this part of
the country, at least, the sweat lodge was very important to us
for healing all kinds of sicknesses. It's where we doctor our
people when they are sick. The Indian people use the sweat
lodge to heat up the blood, in other words. Your blood has to be
heated up in order to get away from all the little tiny bugs—or
whatever you want to call them—this sickness in your blood or
in your system. The sweat lodge was there to protect you from
those sicknesses getting into you, or else to get them out of you.
Today the white man uses a machine to pump your blood into
another machine and from there back into your system again, to
get the heat into it. The sweat is what the Indians have done for
thousands of years, relying on spiritual power.

Maybe sometimes I'll take someone in there who's sick,
with a very few other people, and pray for that person. I have

seen a lot of miraculous things happen in sweats; that is, you can't see it happen, but when you come outside, then you believe it.

We have to use water, we have to use rock, we have to use all the herbs that we put in there for different kinds of sickness. The rocks, the water, the prayers, and all the herbs that are used in the sweat are totally secret. Those are things about which I don't want to be the one to come out and say, "We use this one for that thing." I'm just giving the surface of the whole thing—that we use the sweat for sacred things. We use it for doctoring, and we use it for healing—not only for healing the human race, but for healing everything that's out there, because Spirit comes into the sweat lodge, such as the buffalo spirit, eagle spirit, bear spirit, you name it. They come into the sweat. For when our minds are together—and this is why I have to have another

spiritual person in there too, so that my thoughts are with theirs—they understand what I'm doing, and that way the animal spirit will come in.

That's the way we brought to the surface the teaching that we need to take care of what we've got. We've got to follow the rules and regulations that were charged to us at the beginning of time—how to take care of things, what we should be doing, and so on and so forth. I haven't been really strong explaining a lot of these different things, but I do know what they are.

There was a reason why our sweat lodge was outlawed, along with all our doings as a Native people, what we used to do when we'd gather and have our powwow, as you call it today. The sweat lodge is not a powwow; this is where we get together with all the spirits out there to talk to them, to get their direction, to understand what they're asking us, telling us, to do. But the government came along and said, "You guys are doing evil things." So, they outlawed it.

Photo: Hawkeye Haven

The same with our doctoring. Our doctors, our spiritual people, used to doctor each other or whoever was sick. Then the government outlawed that, telling us, "You guys are doing evil things. If you keep doing that, we'll take you to jail." I have personal experience of that. My uncle was doctoring someone who was really sick. The Bureau of Indian Affairs took him out and put him behind bars. That's how my people explained it to me.

For twenty years we had no sweat. But today we see the sweat lodges that were built at one time; they're still there, and now we're beginning to come back to the sweat. And wouldn't you know it, the white man is doing a better job of it: he's got a torch inside of it—he's got a water faucet inside, and so forth. Then he pushes a button to hear some music. But we Indians, we're out here today, doing what we're supposed to be doing, in a poor way, in comparison, looking like we don't know much about it.

Photo: Nancy Clemens

Doctoring at Rock Creek Canyon

*"It's very important for our young people to learn the Native way,
the way we used to heal ourselves at one time.
We didn't have pills. We didn't have needles.
We didn't have this or that. We were out here,
and we had to rely on what was out here.
That's how we healed ourselves for thousands of years."*

As for the purpose of the sweat, my people have always said that whenever you talk to people, put a joke in there somewhere, so people will laugh, feel better, and so on. Crying is the same way. Each and every one of us cry. When you do more crying, you feel better. It releases all that tension within you. Sweat clears your body; it clears your mind. And that's what the sweat does. I hope you understand what I'm saying.

Sometimes when you go into a sweat, they don't open the door, and you just have to go through the whole thing. But nowadays when I'm working with different people, who don't always know about the sweat, I have to be concerned with their feelings—the way they feel inside. I don't want anybody to be hurt and say, "I'm not going into the sweat any more because it was too hot." We don't want that to happen. We want people to come back and say, "It felt good in the sweat, and I'd like to go back in it again." Myself, I have seen it so hot that when you come out, your nose is burned, your ears burned, and your shoulders—but that's not the way it should be. When I run sweats for different people, I try to keep the focus on what the group is doing by coming together. When people come out, they feel a little different the next morning, and if they keep using the sweat, they will continue to feel a difference, and this is why we take care of it; we don't misuse it.

Sometimes I have had people come into the sweat during a healing. The next day they feel real good about what happened the night before. They might think they were kind of in the way, but they weren't—or that it was really too hot and so forth, but it wasn't. The doctoring in there is what was really important to me and to the people who were sick in there, especially when they feel good the next morning.

Now when there are a lot of sick people in there, if you're a gifted person, you can get it all. In other words, you can get all the sickness if you're trying to do something with it. If you're a gifted person, and you're out here doing what you can to help, all the sickness comes to you—which you have to get out of your body.

These are very important lessons for the young, gifted people. They may be learning it, but they need to rely on somebody else who understands. It's very important for them to do the sweat, and it's like any other test that we go through. The Creator tests us while we're here on Earth. What can we do to save things, what can we do to work together? Those are the tests we go through. Everyone on this planet Earth today, we all have some kind of tests to go through. It's not that we just happened to get sick in the sweat, or because the sick people were in it and so forth. We have to take care of what we've got right there in the sweat. It's the only medicine we have had for thousands of years.

I like to hear a lot of questions about the sweat, because that's the only way people learn. I have run little tiny kids' sweats, and explained to them why we do it, what it's meant to do, and why our people have always done it. Sometimes they ask questions you would never think about. It's a very great experience for me to sit with them and explain things to them and show them how it's done, such as you can't put too much water on the rocks, and so on. Then I open up the door for a while and let them ask questions.

It's very important for our young people to learn the Native way, the way we used to heal ourselves at one time. We didn't have pills. We didn't have needles. We didn't have this or that. We were out here, and we had to rely on what was out here. That's how we healed ourselves for thousands of years.

The herbs out here were our medicine. The tea we still use, some of us, and now, as I see it, the white man's beginning to

say, "Hey, your chaparral out here is for cancer." It is for cancer, but the Indian people have to talk to it. It won't work without the words from the Native people, because they are the ones who are connected to the spirit of the chaparral. Now I've seen them selling those herbs in stores, and maybe they work, but I don't think they can. I have seen them not work on three different people that I know of. But when the Indian people went out there and got the chaparral, within thirty days they got healed up.

When I tried to talk about this to my own people, I told them, "If you're going to use something like this, your minds have got to be connected with it, with whatever you're using. You can't have your doubts," and so on. This is where the problem lies today—the doubt about the power of the herbs. Then again, nowadays we all seem to have doubt about things; we can't always get away from it. A miracle thing can happen, but in order for it to happen, you are the one who is going to have to allow it—in your mind. We are the ones, ourselves, who work with the Spirit. Somebody else can't do it for you.

Like myself, running the sweat. All I do is run the sweat. When I'm praying for somebody in the sweat, when I'm doctoring somebody, then I have to work from the outside. The spirit from out in the surrounding area tells me what to do, what kind of herb to give them, and so on. This is hard for people to believe, because they don't understand that there are spirits of all kinds of animals out here, or that those spirits are who I listen to. They're the ones who are telling me what to do. All I am is just their interpreter.

There are a lot of different things that are hard to understand. This is why I say we are going to have to come back to the Native people's way in order for us to continue, because the Native people are the ones who are connected to what's out there in nature.

For instance, an eagle might fly around when I talk to the spirits out there at Rock Creek canyon. The eagle comes in from one particular direction. He makes a circle there, makes two circles, and then circles back overhead. Those are the spirits talking to him and directing him.

Sometimes people ask me why I use, for instance, twenty-one rocks to build the sweat, and I might tell them that we use twenty-one rocks because you have ten toes—some people have fewer toes, some have more—and some people have five fingers on one hand and maybe six on the other, and it's all according to that!—but then, I like to joke around. Actually, the number of rocks varies. I might use twenty-one rocks when there are going to be a lot of people in the sweat, and I don't want it to be cooling off right away.

When you build a sweat, you have to carry your own rock in your own hand—that's the only rock shovel you have, your hand—and the quicker you do it, the better, or you'll get burnt. So, like I say—I like to joke around—though in a "warrior sweat," as they call it, it really gets hot in there. In other words, you burn your face, your ears, your nose, and your shoulders. It's really hot. You can hardly breathe. That's what they call a "warrior sweat," but why they do it, I don't know. Some people can't take it.

When people look at those huge rocks, red hot, they think, "Gee, what are they gonna do, cook me in here?" But it's not that. It's the way we do it. I don't care how hot those rocks are, the way I do it, even if they're cold, coming into the sweat lodge cold, or just very warm, I can still make it hot.

The way I do it is what the sweat's about. And each and every one of us do it differently. In Battle Mountain when I used to run sweats for people, I gave them herbs first. First the herbs had to go around in what we drank, different kinds of herbs; after that, I'd start using my cedars or whatever herbs I had, and I'd tell the rocks why I was putting the herbs there, and why the rocks had come in there, as I've already explained, from their homes, because those rocks had a home down where they were. I had to tell them the reason why I'd brought them over to another place. And from there, when I built a fire, I'd throw my offering on it and tell the fire, "Make sure you take good care of the rocks, because we're going to use you for our health, so we feel good," and so on. And I continue the same thing when I'm in the sweat; I talk to the rocks, the water, the smoke, and whatever.

The sweat is very important for your body. Praying in there is very important, and you can bring in whatever kinds of spirits that we have available to us to get help from, such as buffalo spirit, eagle spirit, or whatever kind of spirit. Usually a buffalo spirit will come in very first thing. It usually comes in from the south. At Rock Creek, most of the time it comes over the ridge.

If the white man would just step back and say, "Hey, we don't know too much about this; we'll let you go ahead and do your thing; we'll learn from it, and at the same time maybe you can heal us. It's been five hundred years now that we've been here, and we've never healed much of anything; all we've done is destroy what we've got"—then maybe we could start taking care of things a little better than we have been.

Spiritual Phonies

What we've been saying for the last fifty or sixty years, in some places the white man is coming in now and saying, "I know about this. I'm a gifted person," or "I'm this and I'm that." Right now, I want to say this is make-believe. We've got a lot of phonies out there, and sad to say that the bad things are sometimes the easiest to listen to first. The good thing, the true thing, is harder to hear, because it hurts. But we all have to listen to the bad thing, and it's easy to go with that bad thing.

As we know, in California, the sweat lodge has been run by white men out there, and they're charging anywhere from $300 to $600 per head. They don't have any power to talk to the Creator; they don't have any power to talk to the Spirit or anything; but they're doing the sweat lodge anyway. Who gets the blame for it? We do. We get the blame for it, that those white guys are doing this and that, while they're making money off of us, by using us as gifted people.

I went to one get-together they had in Berkeley, California, but the people there were not the spiritual people they claimed to be. Their claims were all make-believe. I even told them, "By God, what you're doing is not the way. You can't make believe and connect with what's out there. You have to be connected to the Spirit." It doesn't do any good to say a lot of things if you're not connected with the spirit of things. That's the bad thing about these people.

Today, also, as we know, there's been a Sun Dance going on in Germany. The Sun Dance is run by spiritual people, a man and a woman right at the entrance. But when you go into the arbor, now it's all so phony, because you go in there and dance during the day, and then you come out, run around in the world, and do whatever you want. Then the next morning, you come in again, you have sweats, you have this and that.

Now how can you have a Sun Dance with water? If you are going to have Sun Dance, it's supposed to be done without any water, without anything to eat. You're supposed to have guards out there watching you, taking you to the hothouse and bringing you back. That's the Sun Dance that I saw when I was young. It used to be five days. Now we got it down to three days. Now we got it down to, if you want to dance for an hour, you can walk out and come back again another hour. It's come to be a game, or I don't know what you call it. This is what the white man has done to the Indian people's tradition.

The Sun Dance used to be a powerful, healing thing that we worked with. I remember not too long ago, when my uncle was doctoring a sick man, the police came and picked him up and took him to jail because he was trying to help this sick man. Then, finally, they realized that the white doctor couldn't do anything for this guy, so they asked my uncle to come in again, and they put him down in the basement of the hospital to doctor this guy and get him well. This doctor was sitting in there when my uncle was doing all this, asking a lot of questions. My uncle never paid any attention to that, never even answered him. You see, your gift comes from your blood, from way back. You don't just pick it up; you don't learn it. There's no way that you can learn those things. You have to connect with the Spirit.

So, not every Sun Dance is powerful. You can do the motion like everybody else, and just do it because everybody else is doing it. But it's where you're supposed to get the power to heal the sick. I remember three different occasions, when a man was brought into a Sun Dance, and they laid him over in the middle pool, and this is where the power was. He laid there for two nights, and by God, the third night he got up. He walked out of there on his own. Three times I have seen that happen, how powerful the Sun Dance was at one time. But not anymore.

Today, the things that we use, the Spirit that I use strongly today—the three important ones like the eagle, the buffalo, and the bear—their spirit is also contaminated with chemicals, and they are getting weak. I try to think about what they tell me. Sometimes they don't want to say anything. Our water, too, is very important. The spirit in the water should be strong, but it's not.

We've got too many of these kinds of phonies running around today. It makes it kind of tough for people to know who the true spiritual people are, I don't care what we do, because the money is there for those people. On the other hand, those of us who don't have money, we can't do anything to bring this out on the surface. That's one reason why I like going on camera, on the radio, and so on, because it's the best way we have to show our people and the whole world the truth, what is going on, and what this is all about, so that we can get real change.

The Way of the Newe Sogobia Natives of Mother Earth

People of the Land

The Shoshone people, as we call them today, are Natives of the land. They come from wherever there is land. They come from throughout the country, all the way from what we now call Colorado, clear across into Wyoming and Montana, into Idaho, Nevada, and California—that's what the white man today calls Shoshone country.

Newe means "native," and he's all over. *Sogobia* means "Mother Earth." Wherever the people roamed, wherever they were at, that was Shoshone country. The Shoshone were all over here at one time—we're going back thousands and thousands of years—they roamed from one end of the country to the other. It's something we can't really understand—why they roamed so far—going into a country like Idaho to get their salmon, and traveling back to Colorado to get their buffalo, and so on. The buffalo used to roam here in this part of the country, but the Newe wanted to go further to get a different kind of meat. It's the same with all the animal life today—they go from one part of the country to a different part. They go south in the fall. In the spring of the year they go north. That's the way the Newe people roamed the country, from one end to the other, during all the seasons, because they had to rely on what's out there.

Each season has a different kind of food that comes on. They traveled to the south for the little berries in that part of the country and the roots. When it became hot in the south, the berries would dry out, and so they would come north, and as they would come north, there would be a different kind of food out there. That's why they traveled from one end of the country to the other, at one time.

They knew the land. They understood the land, where the water is and where certain kinds of food are. That's why they traveled in a band. They would have maybe a hundred or so in the band, and they'd travel together from one end of the country to the other. Wherever they'd dry their food, maybe they'd stay there for a few days, maybe four, five days to dry the food or the roots that they gathered. They'd make them into powder, then at the next camp, they'd dry them over rocks, or whatever. They knew the country well. They knew what was here, what kinds of food, what was best for them to survive on.

They knew these things because they had traveled the country before for thousands of years. They knew where to go, just like the animal life today knows where it's going. They knew where the good springs were, where the hot springs were, and so forth. When they traveled from one end of the country to the other, they knew where they'd be able to cook with hot water, and that's where they'd go to take a bath in hot water and mud.

They understood that it's very important for people to follow the rules and regulations of life. Those things were told to them by their ancestors—what they should be doing, and how they should be taking care of what they've got.

The Indian people would survive on the big red ants, what we call red and black ants. They gathered them in March and then they gathered their eggs, and this is how they made their pudding—out of the eggs. The same with the black part of the ant—they'd separate them over charcoal in order to make soup out of them, or gravy, whatever you want to call it, and that's why they had to pray to the ant hills.

There used to be quite a few ant hills, but there are very few nowadays. You can't hardly find them, because we haven't been praying for them. Not only the ant hills, but there are a lot of things out there that we haven't been praying for, and that's why their roots are not out there any more. The food that the Newe used to survive on at one time is beginning to dry up and disappear.

They were told how to survive on the ant, what the ant will do for you, and what kind of strength he'll give you. The same thing with the eggs in those ant hills. When you get those ant eggs, you can make pudding out of them, or you can dry them up, like powdered milk today. You dry it up, then you put water in, and it will turn white, the color of pudding. Those are some of the things the Newe knew. A lot of things have gone off the face of the Earth, like the natural sugar that used to be all over, but it isn't here anymore.

There are a lot of things out here to eat. The sagebrush has tiny balls on it. That's what they used to make soup out of, with something else mixed in, like deer meat, jerky, or whatever. The hotter it got, they'd continue farther north, and then farther north they'd travel to higher country where they had lots of food that they could survive on. They knew this because they'd been told all this from the beginning of their lives. Their people told them what to survive on, how to take care of it, and so forth. Now we've lost our ways, and we're trying to pick them back up again.

We've got to pray for every living thing out there . . . in order for our food to come back on the face of the earth. Like our chokecherry for one: it's a very important food for me and you, that's supposed to take care of our blood, our heart, and all the bad stuff within. These are important main foods we had for a long time, but they're disappearing. We do see chokecherries in little spots here and there, but they don't have any meat on them; they're just nothing but shell in it.

The same with our pine nuts: they're drying up; they don't have any grease in them. The grease part is a very important part of the pine nut; that's what keeps your health, keeps your system working. They're not all over like they used to be because we have not been praying for them. We took the white man's road which was easy—all we had to do was go to Safeway and pick up what we want. But we don't realize how important it was for our health, for all the living things out there.

The first Shoshone knew these things because their knowledge came from watching the animals. The animal goes out there and digs for its food. It's nature's way of life since the beginning of the Earth. How long has the Earth been here? How long has the human race been here? Right from the beginning, all the human race was taught by animals. The animals are the ones who taught the people how to survive, what to do, and so forth. Animals are the ones who really are taking hold today; they have to survive on the food they find nowadays, and it's getting pretty scarce. That's how the Shoshone people lived. They had to rely on what was out there.

Today, we're still doing the same thing that our ancestors did. That is, we are praying for everything that we get off the Earth, in order to bless the food, in order to bless the water. We have to ask anything that we get off the earth to be blessed in such a way that its kind can continue its life, so they can continue to feed us and give us nourishment.

The Four Seasons

The Native people never stayed in one place very long; they continually moved on with the seasons. The seasons are the reason they kept moving from one place to another all the time. At one time our people had four different ceremonies for the four seasons. February and March is when our ceremony starts. In February and March, that's the time to talk to the snow, for all the little bugs on that snow, to ask them all to make more water out of that snow.

Some people might have noticed that when you pick up snow, or when you disturb the snow, there are little tiny black bugs there. They're the ones that make the water. But today, for the last several years, I haven't been seeing those bugs any more. We have killed them off. It's very dangerous what we're doing to this planet, because we're monkeying with this nuclear poison that's affecting the whole world.

In February and March, when the Indian people got together for the ceremony, they'd remove the snow where they'd have their dance. The circle dance in this part of the country is very important because, as I heard a lot of our people say, "When you dance, you move the ground. You're stomping the ground; that way, you're with the soil." It's very important for Native people to do these things, such as our dance. We mustn't get away from these things, but somehow we've been forgetting them, turning away from them.

Now I see a lot of white people wanting to join in. In Utah, we had a big circle dancing, and they wanted to continue to dance on, but the youngsters had to be in bed at a certain time, so we stayed up only until eleven that night. Now the white man is out there doing our dance better than we're doing it ourselves.

Then in April, our forefathers got together and had another ceremony, when they planted the seeds. The last time I saw it done was in Austin, Nevada, when the two spiritual leaders were out there planting different kinds of seeds—and not this seed you buy in the store—this was the seed that they had gathered in the fall of the year before. April is when they plant the seeds out there. When the spiritual leader does that, whatever seed they plant will grow all over in that part of the country, whatever country they plant it in. That's why I used to have a spiritual gathering in April, but we got away from that practice because it was too much work. Now the white man is encouraging us to keep up these practices, but it's very hard for them to connect with what's out there. They keep thinking they can connect, but they can't.

The people used to get together again in June. This is when they'd bring the moisture from above, when they'd water or dampen their seed.

Then, everybody knows that August is the harvest time, when we'd harvest what we had planted out there. We had to follow the moon, however the moon sets. The new moon is always when we begin, because the new moon is fresh. We, too, had to be fresh, we had to be clean, and so on. That's why our sweat was built—to cleanse ourselves before we begin.

We, and the young people of today, are going to have to unite together to bring the ceremonies back in order for all the living things out there to look at us and be with us.

All the living things on this planet today understand the rules and regulations. However, once we break that law, then the birds and whatnot begin to take everything out there. For instance, when you see a beautiful tree with a lot of berries on it, and you touch it, just to taste them, that way you break the natural law—then the birds and whatnot go after it; the next week there's nothing left, because you're the one who broke the law and got that tree dirty. After you touched it, the tree didn't want to support that energy any more.

We gather the herbs in the fall of the year because that's when they have the power within them. Once the seed gets dry, the powers are inside that root or whatever part we gather. Anything we dry at that certain time of year when things are supposed to be dried, won't spoil. We dry all kinds of berries and so forth. But if you do it in the springtime, or just any time, they get wormy, they get rotten.

It's the same with the ants in March. When the Indian people eat the ants and make the gravy out of them, that's the time they have the honey or the power in the black part of the ants. Everything has a season for it. The Indian people knew the seasons and moved according to the seasons.

In the months of November, December, and January, during the winter months, that's when we'd tell our stories, when the big animals are taking their snooze, in other words. Our belief is, as a Shoshone people, that when we tell stories, that's when the spirits that talk to us come through. Then in February it all starts again, the same prayers and ceremonies over and over.

The people roamed from one end of the country to the other. They'd go down to Idaho, and to Yellowstone. They'd get their salmon, and trade whatever they had. They'd always go south before the fall of the year, just like the animals go south and then start migrating back in the spring, slowly.

Rock Creek Canyon

"We first started coming out here to have our spiritual gathering because we read in a newspaper about the plan to build a dam. Now I have seen a reversal from several years ago when I came here. Now there are more birds flying around, more animals, and fish in this water, and the water seems happier. The air seems very good for the birds and for everybody else.

Photo: Paul John Miller/Black Star

"A few years ago I really missed these things, such as the frog, for one. You didn't hear any frogs. But now you see a lot of frogs, and the same with birds. I see all kinds of birds, and I see animal life in the water. I enjoy looking at them, and I enjoy seeing what they're doing. We can see those things happening here, and it tells me that we are picking up where our forefathers left off."

The people would come through Nevada and Rock Creek Canyon in the spring of the year. They camped at what they call Middle Creek; there's a spring that runs there, a lot of water coming out of that mountain. There was an Indian camp at Midas. They hunted and survived on woodchuck, or rockchuck or groundhog, whatever you want to call it, a very important food for them.

So the people noticed many different things out there. For example, those little black bugs that are in the snow during February and March—the Indians pray for them to make the water. Also, in the spring of the year, the sage hens get fat. What do they get fat on? I never could answer that question. I always thought, by God, they're eating up those little tiny creatures in the snow. I don't know. What else would they get fat on?

And then that groundhog—he'll come out in early spring, but just a while later the big ones go back in. Do they really sleep that long? And the rabbits, we see a rabbit change colors in the winter months, during the snow. The weasel changes colors too. Why do those animals change colors? Why does the snowshoe rabbit's foot grow bigger?

All these questions, and more, I always had in my mind because I never paid enough attention to my people when they talked about those things. I thought it was all nonsense, but now I realize they were telling me something that I should know, and now, today, I don't know. So today, the animals are the ones we need to look to for help, and who can teach us the original ways.

Rock Creek Canyon

Rock Creek is located in the Sheep Creek Mountain Range north of Battle Mountain in northeastern Nevada. Called in their native tongue, Bah-tza-gohm-bah, or "otter water," Rock Creek flows through a small, ancient canyon and is fed by natural springs oozing out of the earth in the middle of the desert. At the entrance to the steep, rocky walls of the canyon stands the Eagle Rock—a sacred mound that overlooks the entrance. The Shoshone place their sick up there for healing. Just below the canyon is a spring-fed pool in the shape of a heart where they go, sing their songs, and receive their visions and power for healing. Below the pool is the site where the formerly nomadic Shoshone made their transient village for thousands of years.

In recent years, Lander County officials have proposed building a multi-use recreational reservoir/dam that would bulldoze Eagle Rock, flood the canyon, and violate ancestral burial grounds. After spending two million dollars on research and learning that the gravel beds below do not hold water, they seem to have dropped the idea because there is no compelling popular demand. But now, mining interests are moving in and want to dig six, thousand-foot wells, create huge settling ponds, and basically terrorize the environment. In recent years, Corbin has invited people to join him in the spring and summer—to protest the dam and the mining, and to honor the land, its ancestral spirits, to sweat, to pray . . . and to "eat real good."

"This is just one place, one example," he says, "of what is happening all over to Native peoples throughout the world."

Bah-tza-gohm-bah Means "Otter Water"

S everal times a year we gather people together for ceremonies in this canyon. Native people and anyone who is sincere are invited to join us here. We started out as a very few people, but every year it has grown. We gather to pray for what's out here, and to teach the younger people about the spiritual ways of our forefathers.

This is *Bah-tza-gohm-bah*, which means otter creek, or otter water, as the white man would call it. As I say, the Shoshone call it *Bah-tza-gohm-bah*. Our people have used this area for thousands of years, and not only here, but throughout our country, at Ione, at Midas, at Kern Creek, and then another place out of Austin—this is where our people had spiritual gatherings and had their burial sites. They buried our remains throughout the country.

I first came out to this canyon in 1941 with a fellow by the name of Doc Blossom. We rode horses through here at that time, and he explained to me what it was about. We took our clothes off and went into that healing water hole. It used to be pretty deep, up to your chest at that time. This canyon was beautiful. It had a lot of fish and a lot of water from the spring.

From then on, I heard a lot of stories about Rock Creek from the "old timers," as we called them. The old timers are very important to us today, because they have the knowledge. We sometimes said about them, "By God, they're too old; they're old fashioned," and so on, but now we're realizing they're the only people who have all the knowledge of what's taken place here and about how we can survive.

Photo: Nancy Clemens

". . . to protest the dam and the mining, to honor the land,
its ancestral spirits, to sweat, to pray . . . and to eat real good."

Otter used to live here and roam this canyon at one time, but now those things have disappeared from this place. Even the fish are all gone from here. The beavers are all gone. There used to be a lot of deer, antelope, anthills, groundhog at one time, but no more. The people used to survive on ground squirrel and all these little creatures running around out here. And there used to be a lot of wild onions and garlic, and many kinds of berries. I only see one kind of berry in here now, and there used to be oodles of them. We all see today there are no trees, no willows. Willows used to be here at one time, but they're not here any more—because we haven't been praying for all this.

Only in the past few years have we begun to pray for whatever is out here, and now, as I see it, things have just begun to come alive again. A place like this has to be protected. Some of us have to wake it up; in other words, we have to wake up the spirits that haven't been heard from in a long time, or haven't been told they're doing a good job. We have to keep telling them our appreciation.

There is starting to be more bird life in the air and animal life in the water. The fish that were here a few years ago were very small, and now they're pretty good-sized, around four inches long, some of them. I see all the birds coming back, and some muskrats down by the creek. So, this place is coming back alive. The plant life, flowers, and so forth are pretty to look at now, but, a couple of years ago, there were not many flowers at all. I think the reason for it is that we began to get together out here and pray for all the living things.

What I'm hoping to do is keep the spirit life alive here—to keep it so they can continue to heal our people and continue to support what was here before, and above all the people who have been buried here and whose spirits are still here. I'd like to keep them alive so that some day, when I'm gone, they can keep me alive, my spirit. You know, there are no ends to our lives. That's why our forefathers told us, "Take care and pray for those things that left millions of years ago."

The danger is that if we don't bless the ground, everything, then we won't have the springs coming out, and we won't have food. We won't have anything to keep us going. Then we'll all be hit with sickness and so forth. Some of us continue on because we believe in the spirits, we bless the spirits, and so forth. Our forefathers lived to be a hundred or more because they blessed all those things in order to continue their lives.

Wherever you go, in places like these, there are spirits out there trying to hold themselves together. We are the ones with voices, and we have to talk to those spirits, and so that's what we're doing by having our spiritual gatherings. When we get together and pray and talk to the spirits of everything that's out here for a few days, then the spirit is happy. The water is happy. The air is happy, and so on. This practice is very important to the people. Even some white people out there who are gifted, they are here helping us help each other to keep this spirit alive here, so it will have a voice and keep talking to us and helping us. That part is very important to us all.

People were brought here because this is medicine water. It's a medicine canyon, a medicine rock, and medicine water. The people roamed through here and stopped here to get doctored, to doctor each other. All their spiritual people knew that this country is very strong for healing power and the gifted power. Some people can get a gift from here, and so this place is very important for them.

Photo: Linda Putnam

Sometimes we have feelings from what's out there. Some of us have a good, strong feeling from this canyon; you can pick up songs, visions, and medicine from here.

The Native people should be the ones who come here and take care of this canyon; the animal life would appreciate it if they would come back again. The Native people were always with them before.

It's very important for all the living things, for all the Indian people, especially the gifted people, to talk to the plant life. Food used to be here, but it has disappeared little by little. I don't think a person could survive out here now. About fifty or sixty years ago, there used to be a lot of food out here for people to survive on. I think that the last time people were in this canyon was about twenty or thirty years ago, until I started coming out here to wake up my people, so that we can under-

Photo: Nancy Clemens

stand what's out here and start praying again to all our animal friends here, our bird friends, and all the other living things in this canyon.

We first started coming out here to have our spiritual gathering because we read in a newspaper about the plan to build a dam. Now I have seen a reversal from several years ago when I came here. Now there are more birds flying around, more animals, and fish in this water, and the water seems happier. The air seems very good for the birds and for everybody else. A few years ago I really missed these things, such as the frog, for one. You didn't hear any frogs. But now you see a lot of frogs, and the same with birds. I see all kinds of birds, and I see animal life in the water. I enjoy looking at them, and I enjoy seeing what they're doing. We can see those things happening here, and it tells me that we are picking up where our forefathers left off.

This place was given to the Indian people. It was a gift, put here on this Earth for them to continue to take care of all the life out here. We have to continue to pray, and if we pick up those ways again, then we have a chance of getting together and stopping the harmful things that we don't really understand, such as the nuclear testing. I don't think anybody understands that kind of thing. If we can put a stop to that, then we've got a good chance of our Mother continuing to feed us.

I hope my people wake up and start doing what we are doing here in all places like this and start supporting each other. We have to do our own spiritual gatherings in our own areas. That's why I invite so many people to come out here to support us, so that they can understand what we've been doing, and what we're going to have to do to continue to save what we've got left so far—not only here, but throughout the country.

Eagle Rock

This eagle head rock here works with a Spirit, the spirit of an eagle. In other words, the spirit of an eagle works in this place.

This eagle rock is very important to our gifted people. The people with good dreams, or people with good visions, the gifted people, would pray for somebody and put them up on that rock in order for them to gain strength when they were sick. So, medicine people put you up there, and then the Spirit takes over with its healing power to heal you from your sickness, from all kinds of sickness.

They usually put people up there for a few days at a time. Whoever could make it up there, that's where they put them. At one time, you could not come off; you could go up there on your

Photo: Nancy Clemens

own power, but you couldn't come down. You had to be helped to come down. Of course, you can't just go up there on your own. Somebody who has the connection with the spirits has to put you up there.

The water works the same way. The canyon works the same way, too. The same with all the spirits in here. There's a buffalo spirit in here. There's a bear spirit in here, and all the spirits together are really important to the human race today. We have to rely on them to continue our healing power, so we can continue to heal each other as Redskins.

Our people have always come into this part of the country to heal their sick and so on. Also, this is where many of our people are buried. This is the only medicine that they had—being connected with the Earth, and not only the Earth, but all the living things that were out here at one time. Because they were connected to all the living things, gifted people were given this kind of eagle head to use to heal our people with.

Down below the eagle head, maybe five hundred feet or so, is a natural spring pond where they dipped the people into the water to purify them. The Indian people used the eagle head rock and all the healing water down below in purifying, holding ceremonies, and whatnot. Of course, all those Native people are *still* singing and they're *still* praying together, and that's what heals most of us today. It heals whatever is out there.

I have used all kinds of rock in my healing ceremonies in the sweat lodge, including some of the eagle rock here. That's why I sing about the eagle rock, when I sing in the sweat lodge when I'm praying for somebody. I'm always using this canyon here, because it is a gift to me, as I look at it. There are some places where I have to use different things, but here in this canyon I have to use this water here, the rocks here, the eagle rock here, this canyon. I pray for them to continue to support us and to continue to heal us. I always ask all the living things for their Spirit to help us along in our life.

Healing Pond

This water here is a healing water, as we call it. We put people in there. When my forefathers finished doctoring different people or praying for them, they always used this water to clean and cleanse their bodies. This was when the finishing touch was put on.

When you came down off that eagle rock, they'd put you down here in this water. Then, when you'd be cleansed from here, the people would give you advice to do whatever it is you were supposed to do, whether it would be to get yourself clean, or put mud on yourself, or whatever.

Then, during the night, the spirit of the water would tell the gifted people what to do. The people would have to follow those rules, whatever advice was given to them from the Spirit. If you didn't follow the Spirit's advice, then the doctor or the gifted person or people, whoever, they would become sick.

Those are always very strict orders from the spirit of the water, the animal, the plant life, or whatever gave the orders. Sometimes the Spirit tells you to wash in here three times. Sometimes it tells you to dip yourself in here early in the morning before sunrise. Sometimes it tells you to put a lot of mud on yourself and then let it dry on you for an hour, and then you are to come back into the water again. Those are the kinds of advice the spirit of the water gives to people. Then, when you go away from here, you feel good. You leave your sickness here, in other words. The water cleanses you.

The advice or medicine you get depends on whatever kind of sickness you've got, and that's what the Spirit will tell you about, through your dreams, or by saying something to someone who's got more power than you have. Evil has powers, so the spiritual people have to watch out for that kind of sickness in people, and that's why they have advice from the water or whatever spirit is out there.

Sometimes the Spirit will tell you to pick up a rock here, or sometimes it'll tell you to pick up a magpie feather or an eagle feather; it all depends on your sickness. Sometimes you become

Photo: Paul John Miller/Black Star

sick because you didn't take the advice from the Creator, or from the Spirit itself who told you what to do. If you don't do it, then you become sick from it. People sometimes get really sick. Then somebody else has to heal them, so they'll come out of that sickness in a hurry.

You don't get the healing by just dipping in the water and cleaning yourself. You can't use soap and shampoo in the water; it's not that kind of cleansing. It's what your Spirit tells you to do. It's the spirit of the water that cleanses you, heals you. Maybe use the mud, or whatever it tells you to get, from this creek. Maybe sometimes it tells you to get a white crystal rock; you can find those things, or feathers of some kind. Those are examples of what the Spirit tells you. Sometimes it's very hard to find a feather for getting well, but you know you are going to find it somewhere, because the Creator, the Spirit of whatever, has told you that it's what you've got to do.

When you're finished, healed, then you leave the sickness here. The sickness stays here when you leave. The water cleanses itself and then continues on. Sometimes the sickness won't leave you unless you follow the advice of whoever tells you to do those certain things. In other words, it always works if you take the advice seriously.

Nowadays, we've gotten used to a totally different way—going by the book, what the M.D. tells us to do. The spiritual people or gifted people don't have that kind of degree. They've got a degree from nature itself or Spirit itself, and that's why I can't explain to you how it's done, since it's all done through the Spirit that nature has given us to work with.

Today, most of our gifted young people, when they begin to get sick, they don't know what to do or who to go to, because we haven't been continuing the old ways, figuring the new way is the best way, but it's not. The old things, like sagebrush, have been here for thousands and thousands of years. There's no such thing as a new way for them. It's always the nature way or the Spirit way. The Spirit heals through nature itself. The power was put here by nature and the Spirit around this water, and that's what heals you. It's not just going in the water that heals you.

And not just anybody can jump in there. Well, you can jump in it, you can do whatever you want with it, but it's not going to heal you unless you get a spiritual person or medicine man to pray for that water and heal you from it. Doing it on your own, is not going to do you any good, because that's just like playing in this water here; you'll just get wet and that's about all. It doesn't work that way.

You need ceremony for it to work. You have to have a word from the Spirit before it works. It's just like any other medicine that we use. You have to give something to it or bless it before you do anything. Same with this water, this healing pond. It's got to be blessed by the people who are going to do whatever for the sick people. This is hard to understand, but it's how nature works.

The healing pond and the eagle rock are the two healing powers here—if the spiritual people use them the way they were put here to be used. Not just anybody can use them, not just anybody can heal with this water or that eagle head up there. It's got to be done by a spiritual person. The spiritual person is the one who makes things work.

I have been a spiritual person since the day I was born, I guess. I understand these things. And I can see a lot of different sickness and so forth, but it's not for me to be telling people that; it's the people themselves who have to recognize a spiritual person. So far, wherever I go, I've been called upon by my people to pray for them, heal them, or whatever. And so far, I've had very good luck in what I do for my people. I pray for them, and then they come out of their sickness, and so forth. I'm not supposed to charge for my services or anything. I'm doing it all for the Spirits. They tell me what to do.

If I were to turn my back on what the Spirits tell me, or turn my back on the people who call me, then I would become sick. I've been through that a couple of times so far already. I've become sick, and then I have to go to some other spiritual person or people in order to get myself healed again. Those are things I have to watch out for. I can't say too much, because the Spirit out there watches every move that I make. Therefore, I can't, you know, say I'm this and I'm that.

Photo: Paul Clemens

It's the Spirit itself who tells the people what they need to do and who they should ask and so on, and I can't refuse anybody either. Some things I have to do. If I'm a long ways from wherever I have to go, then I can't very well make it sometimes. But if I'm called upon by people who are sick, and they are really relying on me, and the Spirit tells me what to do, then I have got to do it. And the Spirit makes sure that I do get to where I'm going, somehow, some way; it's Spirit work, not my work.

As far as taking care of this place, the people themselves used to come out here and pray for the canyon and then clean the pool, or nature itself does the cleaning. The people came over here and blessed the water and kept it clean. While we weren't doing those things, we got moss and other things growing in the pond, and the sand built up in it. But since we've been cleaning it, some people have been able to use it.

It's not made to be used with soap. It's a healing water, and it can't be misused. You can't just come over and put something in it and figure you're going to get healed from it, like putting some kind of medicine in it, like Lysol disinfectant or something like that. We can't be misusing it that way.

Something here in this place always keeps the water clean. When the water from up above goes down to the pond, or when it rains, or when mud comes through, or snow, the next day you can go and see that something's cleaned it all off nice. I don't care how much water goes through, something here keeps it clean. The Indian people know that the Spirit here keeps everything clean. Even when flash floods came through here, they never bothered that pond. It's hard to explain. When we prayed for all the Spirits here, something used to always keep the pond clean.

Canyon Walls

Some people have witnessed something here: you can hear songs, people drumming, people singing here. The Indians prayed to those spirits to keep them alive, such as those two humans on the wall over there. The people used to come in the canyon here and pray for those human spirits. You can hardly see it, but when you look at it, there are two people standing there in the rocks, looking at each other over that water.

Photo: Paul Clemens

The Indian people in these parts usually prayed to those two humans on the wall there, who watch the water. There's a man on one side, and a woman on the other side where the eagle is coming right over the top of her head—where some white streaks are.

I sing a song about the whole rock here, with all those stripes in it. I sing a song to the rocks, too, about how the Indian people have prayed to those two human beings that were here every time they came here. As Indian people, they prayed for all this, that it's very important to have clear water here, and the clear air that we're breathing.

Cave with Medicine Staffs

The cave here used to be a bigger crevice than it is right now. The people, our gifted people, stored their things in there, their herbs. There used to be two medicine staffs left here in this cave by the spiritual people who used it long ago. Nowadays I don't see them any more. All I see is a couple of willows in there.

The two staffs had feathers on the end of them, and they were stuck way back in there at one time. They are what our forefathers used, the medicine people, the doctors, when they were working on people or having their ceremonies here in this canyon. This is one of the things they used, combined with the eagle rock or eagle head, the healing pool below, and all of what's here—the rocks, the singing, and the ceremonies all combined together for them to use for the sick people. For all those reasons they roamed through here on their way from one place to another.

When they'd leave from here, they'd go north in the spring of the year to another spiritual ground. This is one of their spiritual grounds, and it's also a burial site. We have burial sites here, because people's lives might end here, and this is where they put what remains of their life when they end. So they're here now, and we continue as red people to keep their spirits alive by talking to them, giving them blessings, and giving them acknowledgment that they're here, so that their spirits know that we're here.

Sometimes we hear their spirits or see their spirits here. In the sweat lodges that we have built here, their spirits have done their sweat lodges here with us at the same time. It's very important for my people, the Indian people, to start blessing all

Photo: Paul Clemens

*"Sometimes we hear their spirits or see their spirits here. . .
we need to keep all this alive, because we rely on
all these spirits for our well-being."*

of this, such as the ground, so that we can go on and survive for eons to come. We need to keep all this alive, because we rely on all these spirits for our well-being.

The medicine staffs were here in this cave because they were left here when the spiritual people ended their lives. Those medicine staffs are still connected to whoever owned them, and maybe a spiritual person owned them. They were left here for a reason, and that reason was that the power lays here. They were left here to keep the power here in this area. This is a pretty powerful area. You can feel it by walking directly west from here. The same if you go east, you can still feel it, because it's here in this cave or this crevice. It's a very important place.

This mountain's also got a moaning to it. Sometimes you can hear it moaning and groaning, so you know the spirits are here. Sometimes some of us would hear a song, or maybe somebody talking, or whatever, because the spirits are here.

The Spirit sings songs, and you can hear it singing down in the hole below. The medicine women, Eunice and Florence, once picked up one of their songs from that hole. When Florence and I came out here one time, a long time ago, we were standing out here around the mouth of it when a song came in from the hole. Every now and then I ask Florence if she still remembers that song, but she's old now and says she doesn't remember.

A cold wind, cold air comes out of that lower cave with the voice, and hot air used to come out of that place directly above it. The hole with the cold wind is closing in now. You used to be able to go down inside, but now it's closing in. How can solid rock close in? Nobody understands how this happens.

One time I mentioned those medicine staffs to somebody from the B.L.M. when we were here, and I told them, by God, never to let anybody know what was in there, and they promised me, said we'll never mention it at all. But two years after that, those staffs were gone. They aren't in there any more. There are two sticks back there, but the long staffs are gone.

Those medicine staffs are the kinds of things people look for, something they can use and say, "This is what the Indians used at one time." They make a story out of it. But these are things we have to protect, as Native people throughout the country. Those things were very important to this canyon here at one time—they were how our people healed our sick.

I think at one time all around here the Indian people planted nettles, the plant that burns whenever you touch it. There used to be a lot of grass growing here, which hid this cave, but now, because we haven't been praying for it, it's been dying out. I don't know how far the cave goes in; I never have gone back up in there, because I don't want to disturb the things that were left here by spiritual people. It's not up to me to go in there and remove them or whatever. They are there. Those things were left here for a reason, and I just leave them alone, and I tell people not to bother them. People left them here, so there it is.

I tell people it's okay to go down to the mouth of the cave and look at it, but not to go in and monkey around with anything that's left there. It's a bad thing to do, to monkey around with something that's left there by a medicine person. You might get hurt. You might become sick. Sometimes people have to get sick or have something bad happen to them because it's the only way they realize it.

If you see the spirit move, then you'll realize it. The Spirit does move. So these kinds of things should be left alone, because they've been there for I don't know how many thousands of years, ever since people first came to this part of the country.

Burial Grounds

There are quite a few burial sites around this area. They're here and there. I don't point them out to people, but there are quite a few of them up here. This one particular burial site has been filmed by a lot of different people, even the Bureau of Land Management. As I've been told, this was where a mother and daughter were buried a long time ago. Then somebody came along and piled a lot of rocks through here. The rocks covered the bones, the remains of the humans that were here. This was told to me by several different elder people, that this is how we were buried at one time. There are other burial sites around here, too.

The B.L.M. has told me that they removed the bodies of the mother and daughter from here; in 1952, I think it was, they said they removed them and put them in a museum, but they never did tell me where. At one time they told me the bodies were in the Salt Lake City museum. Another time they told me they were in the Reno museum. I never can seem to get to the bottom of it, because they always tell me I have to write a letter to Washington, D.C., and get the Interior Department to prove that I am the person who should be asking those questions.

We never can seem to get to the bottom of these things, because we're always told that the law reads differently than what we see. We try to ask questions and get to the bottom of it, and then it seems we never can, because as Indian people, we don't have the money to hire lawyers and whatnot. So the only thing I can see to do nowadays is to speak out through a camera, through the media, so that people can look at, or read about something like this. The evidence is here, and we can't be wrong on all this. I've been pointing out to people and to the camera that we are trying to protect the resting places of our ancestors,

Photo: Paul John Miller/Black Star

because they were put here to rest. They weren't put here as people to dig out and put in glass jars and in museums.

So far that's what they've been doing to us throughout the world. Our native or Indian remains always end up in the museums so the public can look at us. They shouldn't be doing this to our ancestors, because they were put here to rest. This is their resting area. They should never be disturbed the way they are nowadays throughout the world. We're concerned people like everybody else; we think about our elder people, our ancestors. It's very important for us not to bother them.

The Indians used to camp all along the creek at the mouth of the canyon. There's one place where the sagebrush grew big, about eight foot high, and the burial sites were along the foothills. Wherever you go, you can see where people have already come and turned the rocks over. I know of a few burial sites through here, but I don't like to point those out, because when the public sees them in films or reads about them, they want to dig them up. They already took two of them away, and on the other side of the creek, they want me to give them permission to go ahead and dig another one out. I told them we'll keep on saying, no. We can't let that happen. This is sacred land.

Developing Sacred Land

Like I say, they always want to put the remains of the Indian people in the museums so the public can look at them. Why the Indian people? They're no different from any other people. We all leave the same kind of remains, the same kinds of bones, and so on. Some of us might be a little older than the others; still, they shouldn't be doing that to us. This is where their life ended, and this is how our old people buried the remains of their human bodies—wherever their life ended, that's where they buried them. As Indian people, we don't have a hearse to carry people to a different area, and we don't have grave markings. The only marking we have is where their resting places are.

Our ancestors and elders told us to remember, to make sure we go over there and bless them every year, so that they can have a good spirit and so forth, but we haven't been doing it. We are beginning to realize that it's very important to our culture and history today, as we see things like this on films.

It's not only happening at Rock Creek or in the Boise Valley; it's happening throughout the world, I don't care where you're at. We're always being dug up by somebody, some contractor or

Castle Rock in Boise, Idaho: In Idaho, another unique area is threatened by plans to build more than 100 homes on ancient burial sites.

"Our elders speak of the sacredness of the Castle Rock. They tell us to be respectful of the Rock and the area because there are spiritual beings and power still here. We are speaking on behalf of our relatives, the Castle Rock, the hot springs, and other sacred creations. We ask that you protect these areas." —Kesley Edmo

To modern day Boise residents, it's Castle Rock . . . or Eagle Rock to the Shoshone, Bannock, and Paiute people who were drawn here by the unique rock formation. For centuries, they brought their sick and wounded to the healing waters of the hot springs beneath the rock. Those who did not survive were buried on the hillsides of this sacred ground.

This unique area is threatened, however, by plans to build more than 100 homes on the hillside. Although an agreement with the developers will preserve some of the Castle Rock property, some of the most important areas are left unprotected. Five acres of burial grounds, trails, and open space are in danger.

"Convicts working in the stone quarries near the Penitentiary have unearthed a number of human bones, supposed to have belonged at some period to the noble red men. A quantity of Indian finery, such as beads, bracelets, etc., were discovered with the bones."
—A Regular Boneyard Unearthed Near the Pen, *Idaho Daily Statesman,* January 22, 1893

somebody who just wants to see what we're buried with. I know that in some areas Indian people were buried with different kinds of beads. If that's what people wanted to know, then they could have asked and found out just as easily as digging up the resting places where people have been put.

We come out to see these people here every now and then. My concern today is to have them left alone, not to be disturbed, not to be moved from their resting places to a different area. We don't move the remains of an animal from its resting place. They are left where they died—that's their resting place. The Indian belief is to leave them where they're at, and this is very important to us.

It's unholy to build houses on the graves of our people. It's unholy to disturb this land. Our people died here. They were treated wrong. They were forced out of here and moved onto reservations. Everything that's been done to the Indian people is wrong. All that the developers see is money in their eyes. It's not right. We've been here for thousands of years. White people have been here only for about five hundred years, and look what's happened to Mother Earth—all kinds of contamination, pollution. We need to open up our eyes and see what's going on here. If we don't, we're all going to be gone. That's the message I want to leave for the developers, that it's unholy to develop this land.

Without respect and without our culture, we have nothing. The Indian people were told to forget about the past, but we can't forget about the past. One of our responsibilities is to protect our ancestors, protect their graves. We can't just go out there and dig them out and move them someplace else. That's not according to our ways. We don't have ceremonies for that. It makes a lot of our elders, our elders back home, angry, because things like this are happening all over, no matter where you go.

Photo: Hawkeye Haven

In a canyon within the high Owyhees, native ancestors retreated to escape the white cavalry. A lava overhang marks the spot where an Indian mother hid her children from the invaders. Records from as late as 1911 in Lincoln County, Idaho show that bounties of $100 were paid for scalps of Native men and $50 for women and children.

So many of our religious sites are disappearing. We try to fight the Government, but it just cannot be done. It takes a white man to do it, for he's the one coming out and saying, "You can't do this to the Indian people." Today our burial sites throughout the country are being dug up, and why?

We talk about "due process." The Indian people have never had due process for this land here. It's never been paid for. They had a treaty all right, but nothing was ever ratified in that treaty. This land, as we feel, still belongs to the Indian people who live in this area.

I'm here standing for the ancestors. If we don't stand up, we're not going to have a future here, not going to have a park here. You're going to be looking at homes, at more pollution, more erosion up here. It's not right. You can see what's happening. We have no water in this town, and maybe this year you might be restricted on a lot of water uses. I'd like to see this place stay as it is. It's holy here yet. But once we start developing, that sacredness is going to be gone.

Indian Camps

You can tell that there are burial grounds here, because an Indian camp is down below, and there's one up above. When you first come into the mouth of the canyon, where it starts by the rimrock, there are quite a few people buried. That used to be a camp for the Indian people at one time, right around the rimrock.

You can see where the camp used to be. A lot of chippings and arrowheads are there too, around the eagle rock. The chippings all came from a mountain about four miles back, where the Indians got their arrowheads, their knives, and so forth. When you break one of those rocks, it'll break into a shard about a foot or so long. When you chip that rock, you can make an edge as sharp as a knife. That's what they used for skinning deer and so forth.

Of course, the Indian people didn't use a knife when they skinned a deer. After they cut it a little bit, then they went from there using just their hands. That's why Indian people had tough knuckles, from skinning things by hand. Today we have to rely on the knife for everything we do, but at one time it used to be different.

Photo: Paul Clemens

Down above the healing pond is where they used to have a sweat; the rocks are still there. There are a lot of springs throughout the area; all you had to do was get all the weeds out of the way. We pray for them to continue on.

Eunice, Florence, and Bah-tza-gohm-bah

Eunice is an Indian doctor woman. She's been doctoring people for many a year. She's over a hundred right now. She's been healing people ever since she was very small. Her mother got her power from right here at Rock Creek and passed it on to her daughter, and this is where Eunice got her songs and really got her power given to her. Her mother was a doctor. Her father was a doctor. They're all Indian doctors, and that's why Eunice still continues on her doctoring.

She's really proud of this canyon. She always talks about it, because her mother and her grandmother are buried here somewhere, and they got their power from here. Eunice knows all about this place, but now she won't talk about it. She would talk about the canyon and never forget about what's here. In years past, she always wanted to come out here, but the young people like myself never realized that it was really important to Eunice's life, and we never brought her out here.

She relies on us to do what we've been doing here together, having morning ceremony, praying for the Mother Earth, having sweats, and being together as a people. It's very important that we do this, because we've been threatened by the dam building project which wants to destroy all this by burying it under water.

I got my power from my people. I get it off the canyon wall, or wherever I'm at. Things sing to me, and that's how I pick it up. The same with Eunice—Eunice got her songs here. Florence, the other old spiritual woman, also got her songs here. They were given songs by this particular canyon, and those songs are with them all the time, but nowadays they sing about the new song that comes from the canyon. That's how the canyon is kept alive, by giving songs out to certain people.

Eunice and Florence both say that we have to make sure that we save this canyon—and it's very important to both of them, because this is the only way we're going to be allowed to live on. They say that everything wants to live a healthy life. They are out here praying in our native tongue for the water and the air that we're breathing, that all the living things here should live on happily, that in everything we do, we should always work

Photo: Linda Putnam

Eunice (left): "She's younger than me, this woman, Florence (right), that's my cousin. They used to call us twins, twin sisters, when we were little girls. We worked together a long time, doing healing work and working together in the sweat lodge and praying for sick people. We ran the Sundance together at Wells for many years. Then Corbin joined us and we doctored with him."

together as much as we can. They wonder why their people are not concerned that we're struggling to save this *Bah-tza-gohm-bah*.

Florence says the same thing as Eunice, but she's ashamed to get out and say too much. I keep telling her she has to get used to it, because talking to people, getting in front of the camera, and so on, is the only way we are ever going to bring these important things out.

Eunice thinks that she can't speak good enough English, and then she gets mad when she tries, and can't say what she means.

Photo: Sabine Sauer

Eunice Silva: "The white people want what belonged to my grandmother, and to my great grandmother, and her folks who were here before. They had the water—that's a holy water here—and these people want that water. We say no, that belongs to us. That's the only thing we've got. You took everything else away from us. Some of the Indians want the money. But us real Indians don't need no money. Even I got no money. I don't need it. I can eat just the same. But that white man comes to me and says, 'Do you want to sell that land over there?' I say no, that belongs to us Indians. You people can't have that water, I said. Then he asks me again. Then I have to holler at him to get away. They think I'm going to say yes because I'm an old woman, you know, I'm over 100 years old. I'm the only one who's left. All the Indian old people are all gone. I'm just an old Indian woman. That's what I am.

"And then my mother's mother and her grandma, they're buried around on that side. But the white people want to dig them up. Why? That's what I say, why they gonna do like that? They took another woman with a baby over here on that side. Then I just sat down and cried. That's no way to do like that to us. Some of the younger ones want the money and we say no. I don't want nothing to do with that money. I told them, no, that land and that water belongs to us.

"Now everything is dry. There used to be lots of spring water, but no more. We used to get a lot of pine nuts before, but the white people sell them for money. You know how much a pound? Thirteen dollars a pound. That's what they get for our pine nuts, and they don't leave us any."

Photo: Nancy Clemens

"Eunice is really proud of this canyon.
She always talks about it, because her mother and her grandmother
are buried here somewhere, and they got their power from here."

She figures she can't talk this borrowed language. She says she can't lay it out, because she doesn't know what to say. What comes out of my mouth is sometimes different than what I'm thinking. That's why the old Native people cannot talk too long. If you keep asking them questions, they'll answer you. But as far as them laying it out like a white man does, they can't do it. I don't think any Native people can really lay it out. That's why Eunice and Florence both tell me I'm the guy who's going to be out there talking to the white man. I'm the guy who's going to keep them in line, in other words.

In our doctoring it's the same thing; they have to rely on me. They keep telling me, you are the one who is going to be telling us what to say, what to do, and so on and so forth, but we'll pass on a message to the Spirit that's coming in, or we'll tell what the

Photo: Nancy Clemens

Florence Vega: "I'm the one who prays for the sick people: Corbin and I and my cousin, Eunice; she prays for them after we get through praying. Yeah, that's what we do.

"Well, we pray for sick people. I have my feathers. I pray for them. I brush them, their bodies, and tell them they're going to be cured. When we go in the sweat, we do that.

"I've been among my people for a long time. They put me here to pray for sick people. I told them I'll do that. I've been told by some elder persons all about it."

Photo: Sabine Sauer

Spirit is saying to us. But we, all three of us, get the same message from the Spirit. After we doctor somebody, then we sit down and go over who saw what, which Spirit said what, and so on, so that we're all connected together somehow. We all get the same visions, the same messages from the Creator, the Spirit.

That's why Eunice always says, "You talk to him; he'll tell you more," even though she'll tell you the message she got. At the same time, I'm scared to talk, and I want them to talk. But they tell me, "We want you to do this for us," so that's what I'm doing. In other words, I'm just their follower. They rely on me and say, "You lead us; you're the one who's going to have to do it."

So here I am, doing my best to keep talking to the people and gathering together in our sacred places. We started with just a few people, and there's more and more of us as time goes on.

Threat to Rock Creek Canyon

The county commissioners want to put a dam on Rock Creek, and we keep saying, no, because this is our burial site. The burial sites are our religious ground where we're supposed to pray together, but the white man wants to do away with it all; they want to knock this Eagle Head out and put a big dam there. Above this place there's no water; right here there's a huge amount of water for part of the year, but it dries up each year. From the canyon on, there are a lot of springs, so that's why the Indian people used to come in here and camp all the way down the creek.

We're protesting that dam. We're saying no to that dam. And we've got a lot of people thinking about it. There are a lot of gifted people coming out here and saying it should never happen. I hope this can continue throughout the country, not only here, but wherever there's a spiritual site or spiritual ground. The Indian people need to really hang together tough, because this is the only life we've got, our only mother, and we have to protect her.

They first wanted to build a dam here in 1951, but they didn't have the money. So then they took it to the voters in Battle Mountain in Lander County, Nevada. They took it to the people here, and to the people who came here from some other area as workers in the mines. So the county commissioner here in Lander County thought they could pass that bond issue through the voters, and they did. They got two million dollars.

They came in here to survey and test to find out how deep it was before they hit bedrock. They went 360 feet down, using their backhoe, all in gravel, but they couldn't do it; they couldn't hit bedrock. So they couldn't build the dam right then because the engineers wouldn't go along with it.

Photo: Paul John Miller/Black Star

Eunice: "This is our water, but the white man wants to build a dam here. They can't do that—that's what I told them. But some of my people are saying different, so that's why I'm talking. I don't like to hear them talk, because they don't care about water, but they need money. You want money, I say, but you cannot live without water. They tell me that I don't know nothing—but our Creator, our Creator is the one who put these things here for us.

"Water is very important for me to fight for, not money. I tell them all, no, they can't have our water.

"Soon our Mother Earth is going to create fire. Fire is going to burn everything. Do they know those things coming about? That's what I told them. The Creator gave us the water, but today we're not taking care of it.

"We're following the white man's way, and this land of ours is going flip-flop. You don't know. But I know. I know that this land is going to burn with fire. What they're copying is the white man's way. They're all talking white.

"Everything is dry because we're not praying for it. That's why I'm always telling my people, the white man's way is not the way. But they're telling me that I don't know nothing. I thought they were Indians, but I guess they're not Indians. They're just following the white man's ways. It's going to set us on fire, and the fire is going to destroy us. That's the reason why we're talking bad to each other. We shouldn't be saying those things, because our land, our Creator, is going to turn against us. It's close by, what's going to happen. I used to think like you do, but today, I'm all alone."

Then they hired an engineer from Reno. He came out here as a consultant, you know, just going along with them and telling them, you guys have got to do this and you got to do that. So this engineer used up one million of the money. Little by little, they ate it away, and then they ran out. Now they're saying that they want to bring this issue back up again. They're trying to use people who aren't here from this area in order to pass it, but the people who live in this area and Battle Mountain said no, because they know that this river dries up for part of the year. There is usually just a very little bit of water here at Rock Creek, with no springs up above; the springs are down below.

The county commissioners and the mining outfit—there's a big mining corporation here—were pushing the issue, thinking that they could build a dam here. The mine is about four miles straight over the hill, or about eleven miles going around it down the road, but they're shut down now, because there wasn't enough gold, it was too far to the vein, and they didn't have any water. The mining outfit was pushing the issue, thinking that they could build a dam here, put a big pump here, and pump the water over to the mine. It's what they call Buttes Mine and, on the other side, Silver Cloud Mine. They wanted to make a big, huge tailing pond, about a mile wide. But we told them, how is it going to hold?, because you're on sand and gravel, and all those chemicals that you're using are going to go right through the rocks.

They were going to bulldoze and knock this Eagle Rock right out—this very important rock to the Indian people. The soil conservation and wildlife engineers came out and looked at it, then had a hearing about it. The soil conservation and wildlife engineers asked the commissioners, "What kind of fish are you guys going to plant out there—mud fish? Because this pond isn't

Photo: Nancy Clemens

going to fill up the way you figure. There is all gravel underneath, and it's going to seep right through." They say that they
want to put a plastic barrier underneath, but it won't help. All
the weight of the dirt settles the ground and stretches the
plastic, and it cracks.

All they actually wanted to do was to take the whole place
away from the Indian people. That's the only logic I can see. So
like I always say, they're taking a little bite at a time, and now
it seems like they're going after the sacred spots, as a way to
weaken our people. They know we become weakened without
our spirituality.

That particular mine isn't operating now. A Japanese outfit
from a foreign country was in there, but they ran out of money.
But there are a lot of other miners throughout the Western states
trying to steal the Indian land by voting on it, and then killing all
the life around them with their chemicals.

Photo: Paul Clemens

And there are mining stakes, mining claims, all around here. But some white people have been coming out here and moving the markers, the 2x4s and boards. People come in from other towns and just knock them over or change the locations. The Indian people are not doing that. It may be just a very few people, but I know that it's taking place.

I'm asking people to support us, to stand against building a dam here at *Bah-tza-gohm-bah.* That's one reason why I keep travelling throughout the country, saying, "We need support." We need the white man's support to put a stop to something that they're going to damage here. Only the white man can put a stop to it, because the white man will only listen to another white man.

Photo: Paul Clemens

I'd like to see everyone writing letters to their congress-men, to their senators, and their lawmakers, stopping all this nonsense that they're doing to our people throughout the coun-try—and not only here, but throughout the world. This canyon and other places like it are very important to the Indian people.

They would like to take our Rock Creek Canyon away from us, and then we would suffer from it. We have to think strongly about this. We were born and raised with this sacred place, and it hurts to see something else take over there. This is not the way it should be, and we have to rely on others today to help us, because only working together as a people can we do some-thing.

The White Man's Way

The White Man's Laws

For years our Native people have been told that what we do—our ceremonies and prayers—are evil things. For example, when I was trying to take my Eagle feathers across the Big Lake (the Atlantic), they thought that through these I have a lot of power and that I can do a lot of things. They don't want me to have the power to do anything; they are the ones who want to have the power to say whether I can have the Eagle feathers and take them with me.

It's very important that the Indian people have their power to do the things they used to. Today we've gotten away from that idea, and we've been trying to establish our power with a piece of paper, traveling to Washington, D.C., and so forth. But it's not going to work. A law on a piece of paper can't change the life of a tree, which way it stands, what it does, and so on.

Now the white man is trying to change this tree by taking away the water. The white man is beginning to say, "Hey, I own this water." Pretty soon they are going to be telling us on our Indian lands, "You can't be using my water." He's going to be sitting there with a gun trying to take your life. That's how important that water is going to be in a very short time—a very short time. It's already happening in some places. I've already seen a man get killed over water. So that's just the beginning of it.

Now, wherever we go, the white man is trying to get the water away from other people. They don't want anybody else to use it. So that's where we're going to be today. They charge us for the water, which doesn't belong to them to begin with. It belongs to the Earth. It was created by the Creator. And they're charging us for it. Everybody is paying for water.

Next will be the air. How are we going to control this air? Pretty soon they're going to say, "Well this here air belongs to me." But they can't control it. They can't control the water either, but they're claiming they can.

The same with Mother Earth. The soil today is owned, like this valley here. Mostly the Mormons own this particular valley, because when they came in, the Indians moved on. They moved from this valley to another valley to another valley, then to another valley, and then they continued to move on. And the Mormon settlers said, "This land here is mine. This is our private property."

So we Indian people began asking questions about that: "How did you get that land?" "From whom?" "When did you come here? You weren't here when our forefathers were here." "You came in from someplace else." "What did you do, buy it over there, or what happened?" This is what took place. But as Indian people, we know this land can't really be owned by just some of us. This Mother Earth here belongs to all of us, all living things. Everything should use it. Everybody. And take care of it.

Divide and Conquer

I call us "Redskins," but people on the other side of the Big Lake call us all "Indians." They don't say we're this tribe or that tribe, they say, "All of you are Indians. You were there when our forefathers arrived. We know you're Indians."

They didn't say, "You're Paiute, you're Shoshone," and so on; they just said, "You're all Indians. You're natives of the land there."

The government and the people over here say to Indians, "You're a certain tribe here; you other people are this tribe over here; and those people over there are that other tribe. That is how they divided us, and today we continue to be divided because we're thinking, "Well, I'm not this one; I belong to the other one."

But we're not really divided. Look at the Temoak for one. The Temoak are divided into five different tribes today. They're all Shoshone, but now they're divided. Come right down to it, it used to be one nation at one time, covering five different states. That was the Shoshone Nation, but now we're saying to each other, "You're so-and-so." We're continuing to divide ourselves.

Today it's worse, because the white man is using money to further divide us. He wants our land here because he can make oodles of money off it. Down in different valleys today, they're making lots of money from mining gold and other minerals. Here, we're the land owners, but what are we doing? We're not even getting the droppings out of all that—nothing. At least if there was a dime drop every now and then, we could get something out of their use of the land, but then money is not our concern as a red people. Our concern is how we can save our Mother Earth. That's more important than money, but even our own people have forgotten.

For us, it's really hard. The Indian people are wards of the government. We've never been taken care of. All they've ever done is take our land and use our land, all over the United States. The law is against us. At the same time, they tell us, we'll take care of you, we'll protect your rights, but they're not. They're taking everything away from us. Our Sun Dance just came back within the last twenty years. Before that, it was outlawed. We couldn't do our Sun Dance, because they said it was evil. I could talk about a lot of these things, for days. They set up reservations here and there to divide us, "divide and conquer," as they say. Today we are divided, and today we're not united.

The government told us, "We'll take care of you better if you are put on reservations." But we haven't been better taken care of. That's why our people are divided on a lot of different issues. They don't trust the government. They don't trust anybody. Now the government's using money to continue to divide us through government policies and reservation laws. Each and every reservation has its own particular laws set up. They made those laws so that we're not unified as a people, and they're still doing that, even though we might not realize it.

The white man does not acknowledge the 1863 Treaty of Ruby Valley (see Appendix), therefore their thinking is to take a little land at a time, so that someday they can say, "Well, we took your land from you," without even mentioning the Treaty at all. They try to divide us throughout the country. The Indian people used to live together. Today we're separated, because the white man came in here with their laws and regulations. So today my people don't recognize one another because we're all from different reservations and different colonies—we think. But the truth is, we're all Indian.

The Bureau of Indian Affairs continuously tries to divide us one way or another, by using our "blood quantum"—we have to prove with papers that 25% of our blood is Native—or by using our language against us, so that we are losing ground in their viewpoint by not speaking our Native tongue; by not allowing us to continue our spiritual gatherings and our spiritual practices; and by our not doing what we've been doing now at this *Bah-tza-gohm-bah* canyon. That's how they divide us, and they'll continue to divide us if we don't unite together as a people.

They used us to begin with, from when Europeans first came into this part of the country. They moved us from one area to another, and now they are trying to teach us to go out there and mingle with the white people, to get us away from our land base.

Today we are struggling out there. Whatever we do, we still don't have the same power as any other people would have, because the government, the Department of the Interior, keeps telling us, "You Indians control it, but we hold your land under trust; you are wards of the government," and so forth. They don't treat us as American citizens, because we can't vote. We're held captive as prisoners on our own land, and we have no power and no control. We're government property.

Our people were put out here because it was out in the desert where they thought nobody could survive, and they left us alone for a while. Then after a while, some of those people were shifted to Owyhee, for one, and then some of them didn't want to stay there, so they came back and settled, for example, in Beowawe, which was owned by some lady who said, "Well, you guys can go ahead and use this land." So they built homes on that land and lived there for a while until the Bureau of Indian

The U.S. vs. the Dann Sisters

Chief Raymond Yowell, Western Shoshone National Council: "When the U.S. entered into the Ruby Valley Treaty of 1863 with the Western Shoshone Nation, the U.S. acknowledged the Shoshone's existence as a nation and recognized our rights to our homelands. Our rights as indigenous people were granted to us by the Creator of Life when we were placed in these lands countless generations ago, and not granted by the invading Americans or any of their federal agencies. The Western Shoshone have never relinquished our indigenous rights to the U.S. or any other non-Shoshone government."

The Bureau of Land Management (BLM) reported (2/92) that it has started the impoundment of livestock belonging to Mary and Carrie Dann in Crescent Valley, Eureka County, Nevada. The BLM first filed suit against the Western Shoshone sisters in 1973, alleging that the Danns were grazing their livestock on BLM's Buckhorn allotment without a federal permit. This allotment is within the Western Shoshone Nation's lands, a territory recognized by the United States as Western Shoshone country in the Ruby Valley Treaty of 1863. Because the 128-year-old Treaty is still in effect and has been consistently honored by the Western Shoshones, the Danns maintain that only the Western Shoshone National Council may regulate Western Shoshone ranchers within the Treaty-recognized Shoshone lands. The Western Shoshone National Council is awaiting word from Senator Harry Reid, D-Nev., on the next step toward resolving the Western Shoshone land rights issues.

Source: Western Shoshone National Council and *Las Vegas Review-Journal*

Affairs came along and told them, "We'll put you in a good house; we'll take care of you."

So they moved them again, and after they got their new homes, they were told, "Well, you have to pay rent here." Well, a poor guy like myself, how are we going to pay rent? Little by little, they have taken our lives away from us. Then all over the country I've seen military bases being closed down, and I have hollered about it before. For example, the Indians could use those homes in Indian Springs (Nevada). I've said, "Why don't you give these homes to the Indian people—they can move them." Hawthorne is another place, where there's an ammunition dump; there are oodles of homes just sitting there, just rotting away, but yet the government says, "Well, you know our poor people, homeless, are out there, who don't have any homes." But when we ask the office for a home out there, they told us, "No, it's government property."

Well, so are we! We're government property, you know, but they won't give us anything. So those are the things we experience. This is just one of many, in one little place, and it's not the big issue at all.

Not too long ago, I went to one of their government meetings in Duck Valley, and this is when the Fort McDermitt people were saying they were going to accept the government offer of $200,000 to allow them to come in there with a nuclear dump site. I warned them at that time that the $200,000 had already gotten them hooked, that once the D.O.E. has their foot in the door, they are going to open it a little bit wider, and that they were just going to shorten their lives.

"What the D.O.E. is going to do," I said, "is come onto your reservation somewhere down the line, and kick you guys out,

remove you off that reservation, and take it away from you."
Then I asked the government people if I was right by what I was
saying, and no one said anything. They said, "All we do is get
orders from higher up."

We're all involved in it. The Air Force told us once before,
"We can always remove you Indians elsewhere."

These things have happened before, and they're going to
continue. This is what we have been through as Indians.

Blood Quantum

As Native peoples, we get stuck on the white man's law
because we don't understand it. For example, we are the only
people on this Mother Earth who have to have a blood quantum.
If you understand blood quantum, that is how you tell what kind
of a horse you've got. Your horse has a certain amount of blood
value depending on what stock he came from. That's how we've
been treated for a long time, like horses, and in fact, we're still
at that stage today. What they're saying to us now is that if
you're a member of a tribe that is recognized by the federal
government, then you fall within the law, but if you are not,
then you're just nobody. They say you have to have so much
blood percentage before they recognize you as an Indian. Under
a certain quantum, you don't have any Indian rights. I've seen in
Duck Valley where two brothers or two sisters have been
assigned a totally different blood quantum.

I've asked a lot of people about these things. You see, they
dial a little wheel. There are three people sitting there, and
they're supposed to be the ones who determine your blood

quantum; they spin that wheel. Wherever it stops, that's your blood.

Then, if you don't agree with it, they pass it on to the next person, so the next person spins the wheel again, and whatever it stops at, that's your blood quantum. After a while, they want you to be nothing, not human at all, I guess. It's very dangerous what they're doing to the Indian people, and we have to recognize as a people that we're *not* different from each other.

Discrimination

My people are a shameful people. They cannot seem to come out from behind the bush. It's where our problem lies today. People who have been mistreated for a long time still remember those things. In the back of my mind are still thoughts of my people who were slaughtered. I've got documents that can stand here before you and say where people have been slaughtered. Their scalps were worth a hundred dollars when they were brought in—as recently as 1909—and scalps of women and children were fifty dollars.

But when the story came out in your history books, it was reported the other way around, that we scalped you white people. We didn't. We didn't know how to, to begin with, I don't think. We were scared of death. We didn't want to hurt anybody.

Our people long ago never used to have hard feelings towards the non-Indians. To them, we all looked the same at that time. It's very important for us today to forget about all that, to let it pass, and to try to protect all our younger generations who are going to be walking this Mother Earth. That's what we're standing for, today, trying to do the very best for our younger generation, so they'll have a peaceful life to live on the Earth.

We have witnessed lots of discrimination towards Indian people. We were run out of cafes or restaurants; they told us, "You can't come in here. You can stay outside and eat, outside the door." Also, we used to be told never to get on a bus unless there was room way in the back. We were treated that way. In 1941 in Nevada, people were told never to come into a restaurant. They could order from the back door, but they couldn't come in. This was still happening not too long ago.

Nowadays the B.L.M. people threaten the Test Site protestors, telling them they're going to take away their belongings. That's not the law. That's not protecting people's rights. That's just taking away their property and their life, which is just what they did to the Indians.

The Creator has said, "Anything that gets done in a circle," as the Indian people say, "can never be broken." There's a beginning for everything, and the beginning comes from a particular point, and things are going to come back to that beginning. So the Indian people, the Native people of this country, have to stay together in that circle if we're ever going to lead the white man out of this mess we're all in.

Nuclear:
Our One Big Enemy

"With over 900 bombs exploded, the Shoshone are the most bombed nation on Earth."
—Chief Raymond Yowell, Western Shoshone

"We've created a monster, with no means of destroying it or neutralizing its effects, and we have no place to plant it. We cannot put it back into the Mother Earth as it is, since it's not the same as it was when it came out. It's been transformed into a monster."
—Bill Rosse, Sr., Western Shoshone

Photo: Hawkeye Haven

The Thing We Don't Understand

We have one big enemy, a very important one, against which we, the people, have to unite together to stop. That one big enemy is the development of nuclear energy. Nuclear plants throughout the world and nuclear testing throughout the world are going to wipe us out. Once it contaminates our Mother Earth, then Mother Earth cannot produce food for us, or for all the living things on this Earth.

I've been working for the past few years down at the Nevada Test Site. It's on our Shoshone land that they're testing those nuclear weapons. They're using our land for bad things. I've been working with the white people against the Test Site, and the Native people in this part of the country are also saying, "This can't go on." Everybody's beginning to realize this. Forty or fifty years ago, when it started, everybody was hush-hush about radiation danger—until we experienced the effects, and it started taking over our lives.

So our role is in a dangerous place to be, but we're involved in stopping the testing, and somebody has to do it. I guess I was chosen by the Spirit, so I'm out there talking, meeting people, going on the radio, taking pictures, and making videos—anything I can do to make people aware how serious this nuclear contamination has become.

Between the United States and Great Britain, they've exploded almost 1,500 huge bombs down there. They're telling us it's safe on the surface ground, because the blasting is done way down deep. I and other people are asking the D.O.E., "What is that blasting doing within our Mother Earth?"

I hope that we all can work together as a people to put a stop to it. Sometimes I think it's hopeless. But something keeps me moving in that direction, to shut it down. They shut down nuclear testing in Kazakhstan, Russia, but—except for the moratorium in effect (1994)—the United States and Great Britain still want to test in this part of the country, the French government has done extensive testing in Polynesia, and the North Koreans, Chinese, and others are continuing to test—and that's dangerous for us all. When they set off a bomb blast over there, it goes into the air, and the air carries the radiation around the globe. The same with our water: our water, which we're pumping up from below and bringing up here, is already contaminated from within our Mother Earth.

We have to unite together—as a people—to put a stop to nuclear testing. Nevada might sound like a long ways away

Photo: Paul John Miller/Black Star

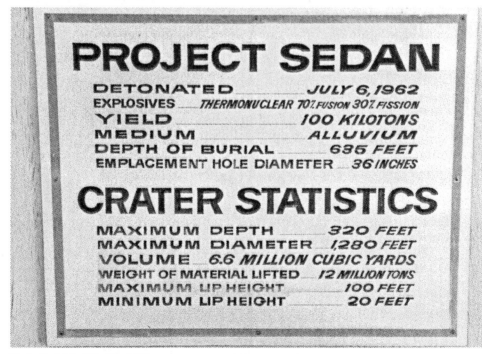

Photo: Paul John Miller/Black Star

Photo: Paul John Miller/Black Star

Text on sign: "It is unlawful to possess, harass, transport, injure, kill, receive or remove a threatened or endangered species."

Photo: Paul John Miller/Black Star

The U.S. Military Invasion of the
Western Shoshone Nation

from some people's homes, but it's not—the air that we breathe today, is already contaminated. The wind patterns have carried that contamination to all parts of the country and beyond.

The nuclear testing they do within the Earth, drilling holes into it, a mile or two miles deep, and then blasting away—what do they think it's doing to the water table underneath? What does it look like underneath us? We've only got one planet; we've only got one air, one water. So what is this testing doing? And what is the effect? The government people will now admit, "We don't really know."

There are three small towns in northern Nevada where they're already hauling water in because they can't use the water that is there. In Carlin, Nevada, one of those towns, they've already been told, "Your water is contaminated; boil it." But boiling it won't work. Wherever we are, we're going to be drinking the same water that we're drinking here, and breathing the same air. There's no other planet that we can move to; this is our only home.

The soil that we're standing on says to us, "Take care of me, and I'll take care of you." That's what it's said for millions of years, as long as the planet has been here.

Our land is suffering on account of nuclear testing and uranium mining. We have to preserve this Earth, rely on this Earth to give us food, clothing, and all the luxury that we have. Everything is here for us to use, but nuclear energy is not the way to continue with what we have. We don't understand radiation or how the release of nuclear energy is affecting the Earth. Our forefathers didn't know anything about it, and our medicine people don't know how to cure people from it.

In our part of the country, the fish don't have any sort of solid meat to them. They're as soft as can be. Every lake in this

The Western Shoshone Nation calls upon citizens of the United States, as well as the world community of nations, to demand that the United States terminate its invasion of their lands for the evil purpose of testing nuclear bombs and other weapons of war.

Photo: Paul John Miller/Black Star

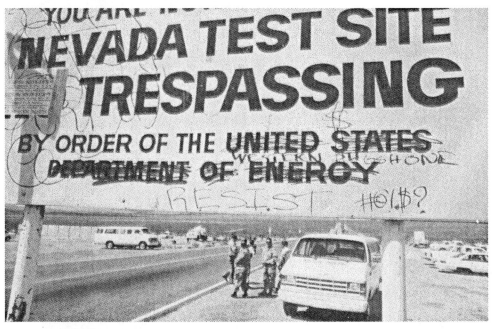

Photo: Paul John Miller/Black Star

Photo: Linda Putnam

Healing Global Wounds Ceremony, October, 1992, Nevada Test Site

Photo: Linda Putnam

Nuclear Testing stats: As of 1991, the U.S. has stockpiled over 20,000 nuclear warheads, costing hundreds of billions of dollars. Nearly two billion dollars were spent during the 1990 fiscal year on research, development, and testing of nuclear weapons.

Since the 1940s, the U.S. has spent $300 billion dollars on designing, testing, and manufacturing approximately 60,000 nuclear warheads. The warheads contain 90 to 100 tons of weapons-grade plutonium and 500 tons of highly enriched uranium. Similar stockpiles are believed to exist in the former Soviet Union.

Atmospheric nuclear testing has left a legacy that, according to a recent medical study, will result in 430,000 cancer deaths by the year 2000. Since 1963 undergound nuclear weapons testing at the Nevada Nuclear Test Site has contaminated the environment, groundwater, and communities of the Great Basin. The grand total for international nuclear tests since 1945 is 1,910.

—Source: American Peace Test

country is affected by radiation or chemicals. So we know it's having an affect. The time is coming when the people from Nevada and the "Downwinders" of Utah, Idaho, and Montana will show us what is happening all over the world, wherever nuclear testing is being done underground—what damage this is causing inside the Mother Earth.

Our water in the lakes comes from springs in the first place. Once those springs and underground lakes are mixed with that dangerous something else, then all our water is going to be dead water.

My people have always said that, when water becomes dead water, you can't revive it at all. That means that everything out there is not going to survive without that water, because the water's got to be alive. It's got to have a spirit. Once you kill that spirit, you have nothing. Once we kill the spirit of what's out there, then we are at a standstill.

Bill Rosse, Sr.: "This here permit is to allow you to come onto the land at our request and as our guests, and this shows the government that they don't have a right here. According to the Treaty of 1863, this land is all ours. The people out there doing all this damage, they don't have a permit from the Shoshone Nation. They never had permission, and we feel it's the wrong thing what they're doing out there. It doesn't go according to our beliefs and our religion."

When I was young, the elder people used to talk about these things, but I never paid much attention to it, because I was too busy doing something else. Today we're seeing what they used to talk about: today, our Mother Earth is suffering. Even now, our food is starting to have something foreign in it. Some of our plant life has disappeared, along with some of the little creatures

January 5, 1991, prior to direct action at gates of Nevada Test Site:

"The Western Shoshone are the rightful custodians of this land, affirmed by the 1863 Treaty of Ruby Valley," says Chief Raymond Yowell. The Department of Energy claims it purchased the land from another government agency, the Bureau of Indian Affairs, but the Shoshone have never agreed to sell their land. "Now, Shoshone, Paiutes, and other downwind communities suffer from cancer, leukemia, thyroid problems, and birth defects.

With over 900 bombs exploded, we are the most bombed nation on Earth."

that live in the forests. This nuclear power is going to wipe us out as a human race, along with all the living things on this planet.

We know that what they're doing at the Nevada Test Site is a very dangerous thing. And what about that nuclear waste generated by the nuclear power plants? We have attended meetings where they discuss how to transport this waste from different parts of the country to another. But they don't know where to put this waste. They keep saying it's going to be here or there and so forth. I went to one meeting in Spokane, where they talked about transporting the waste from Hanford, Washington through Burns, Oregon, then from Oregon into Winnemucca, Nevada, from Winnemucca into Battle Mountain, and then over through Austin into Yucca Mountain through Tonopah. Another route they talked about was from Burns, Oregon into Bruno, Idaho, and then coming through Duck Valley Indian Reservation and over.

Those things happen in our part of the country all the time. They try to go unnoticed, to do these things in secret, but we know about it, and much more. Then they ask us advice and do environmental reports, and even when they're told that a nuclear waste dump site at Yucca Mountain is unsafe, they want to go ahead with it anyway (see Appendix). Even so, they say they are planning waste storage for ten thousand years, but the life of that waste is millions of years.

A man who worked in the valley told me that he and his father before him worked there, and that they both came down with sickness. They tried to sue the D.O.E., but they couldn't do it, because when you work for those guys, you make an agreement: they make sure that you can't go against them in court. It's just like going into the Army: when you sign on that dotted line, you cannot go to court against your government. They've used that same trick on us Indians for many a year, as wards of the government, with our blood quantums, and the way they divide us on reservations.

I used to talk about nuclear dangers in Idaho Falls (Idaho), when they first built that plant there. I told them at that time, some day you are going to find radioactivity in the Snake River, because your rock is not solid; it's got lots of crevices in it. Then

Bill Rosse, Sr., on the 1863 Treaty of Ruby Valley:

"According to the Treaty of 1863, this land was all ours. We gave the government the right to come across the Humboldt Trail, over the northern part of Nevada. It gave permission to pass over unmolested. This is what the treaty was, a Treaty of Friendship, and it's also called the Treaty of Ruby Valley.

"We gave them permission to pass over, to build support stations there if they wanted to. But we didn't give them all the land. That was land we were supposed to be caretakers of. Some way or another, the government claims to own it now, and they really haven't shown us any way that they can own it, because we couldn't sell it to them.

"They said they bought it in 1979, December 6. They claim that when they appropriated $26 million for damages and other stuff, that it was for the sale of the land. We never accepted this money. The Secretary of the Interior accepted it on our behalf, saying we were too dumb to know what's good for us, and what not. The government took it, and they've still got it. They just transferred it from one hand to the other and said, you've been paid. But they can't say what's really the taking date, for sure.

"They've got an 1872 date when they gave the land a value, but nothing happened at that time. Then in 1934, when the Taylor Grazing Act went into effect, and the Reorganization Act for the Native People, they say that was the taking date. But there's no record to show that. Also in 1979, there's no record to show that we accepted any money, so since we haven't accepted any money, we feel the land is still ours to be caretakers of.

"The government claims that the BLM and the Forest Service are the ones that's letting them blow the innards out of Mother Earth, contaminating the water and the land, and using the people as guinea pigs. These are the things that we're trying to stop. This is the reason we're sitting here issuing permits for people coming onto the land.

"The permit allows people to come over and be on this land with us here, and be a part of us, to walk on our land with us here, and anything that happens here. This is what the permit gives them permission for. And since we've been issuing these from January 1, 1987, they've been releasing all the people that they have picked up for trespassing. They haven't prosecuted any of those cases.

"The government never had permission. They never came to us to ask whether they could test the bomb here, or strip mine as they're doing. President Harry Truman proclaimed it a test site January 27, 1951. We feel it's the wrong thing what they're doing out there. It doesn't go according to our beliefs and our religion. We're supposed to share this here land with all our brothers and sisters, and not contaminate it like they're doing here, and creating a monster out there that will be the destruction of the world. We don't feel that needs to be going on any more.

"Our brothers over in the Soviet Union were able to stop their testing. They've even been trying to help us stop this. They feel that we're going to succeed eventually, because the people will begin to wake up and see what's really been going on.

"So I'm gonna be one of these guys coming around here with a clipboard and giving people permission to be here. So if they want to arrest somebody, they can arrest me, or the Western Shoshone National Council actually, since I'm their representative."

I found out, a few years down the road, a woman wrote to me and said, "Well, how did you know this would happen? Now we are affected by it, in Blackfoot, Idaho." So we're all in this together.

In other words, we're all facing death. When we monkey around with nuclear energy, it's going to take the life out of all the plant life, and out of us, the humans, and out of everything. Life is not going to be here very long if we continue to monkey around with chemical and radioactive things. It might be a quick death for some of us; some of us might have to suffer as we lose our life. It's a sad thing to say—but we all know in our hearts—we know that it's going to happen if this nuclear testing continues on.

Protests at the Nevada Test Site

We started out protesting at the Nevada Test Site because we realized that we need to help the Earth—all of us together.

Photo: Linda Putnam

*Tribal Drum of the First Nations, direct action following
the All Nations Healing Ceremony, April, 1991*

Bill Rosse, Sr., [Western Shoshone Environmental Council] was
the one who started going there, then I came along and joined
him afterwards. I guess he gave me a bunch of candy and told me
to come help him. That's what it took for me to join in. Ever
since then, we've been struggling with it. When we first went,
there were only six of us out there at the gate.

The Test Site officials wanted to haul us over to Mercury
[Nevada] and give us a tour—but then they refused to take the
non-Indians that we invited, because they were out there joining us and protesting this nuclear testing. When we heard them
refuse those people, the chief and I said, "No, we're not going to
go in. We're just going to stay out here and talk to these people
about what they are doing to our planet here."

Photo: Linda Putnam

"Legions of Mercury," Nevada Test Site, April 1991

So that was the beginning of what took place. From then on we started asking a lot of people throughout the country to come out and join us: "Let's put a stop to this monster." At that time nobody really thought much about it. Most people just thought that the government was doing its job to protect the citizens, and that the nuclear testing was to protect this country from other countries.

At the same time, we knew it was dangerous, because our people used to talk about those things. They knew this would happen from way back. How did they know? I really don't know. They used to say, "Protect, take care of what you've got in order to live on: you have to think about all the young people, all the living things out there."

We have been saying all along that it is wrong for the D.O.E. to do what they are doing on that piece of land. Then, as the protests got bigger and bigger—thousands of people came from England, Germany, and Russia to support us—and more people started to realize how dangerous it is and how the people are being affected by it—the sickness, leukemia, birth defects, and losing their lives—still, nobody paid much attention to us. The government people kept saying, "It's not the radioactivity," or "Nuclear testing had nothing to do with their death." They know in their heart that the radioactivity is the reason so many people have gotten sick. But the government never wanted to hear it and never paid any attention to those people. They still don't want to hear it, and the same thing is still going on today.

We have been saying all along that it was wrong in the first place for the D.O.E. to be doing what they are doing on that piece of land. In the Ruby Valley Treaty for Peace and Friendship of 1863 (see Appendix), the government made promises that this land belongs to the Western Shoshone people. Under the treaty, this land was set aside for the Shoshone. But the government didn't keep their end of the bargain, and so my people used to say that white folks talked with a forked tongue. And they still do, today.

Photo: James Lerager

Photo: James Lerager

Photo: John Paul Miller/Black Star

*Mass demonstration and healing ceremonies with groups of indigenous, U.S.,
and international walkers at the Nevada Test Site gates
calling for the end of nuclear testing and the recognition and return
of the test site to its rightful stewards.*

Photo: John Paul Miller/Black Star

Photo: Paul John Miller/Black Star

Photo: Paul John Miller/Black Star

Photo: Linda Putnam

Arrest of Chief Raymond Yowell at Nevada Test Site, March 1988

Photo: Linda Putnam

Parade of the Atomic Veterans and Radiation Survivors
Direct action following the All Nations Healing Ceremony, April 1991

Photo: Linda Putnam

Healing Global Wounds Rally and Forum, October 1992

MESSAGE TO THE INTERNATIONAL CITIZENS CONGRESS
FOR A NUCLEAR TEST BAN
from Corbin Harney,, Western Shoshone Spiritual Leader
Newe Sogobia, "People of Mother Earth"

Alma-Ata, Republic of Kazakhstan, U.S.S.R.
May 24-26, 1990

The U.S. and the U.S.S.R. have to realize we are only one planet. We breathe the same air. We need to warn the young people. It's all on our shoulders. We have to create a good thing. We're not going to say, "I wish we would have done something." There's no ifs, ands, or buts. We've all got to stick together. Everything is relying on us.

We know there are animals out there that are gone. The frogs and polliwogs are dying out. There's acid rain. We are the ones doing the polluting. All the tiny insects out there doing their job, they're gone. We are going to be with them if we do not clean up our garbage. We have created problems for our sun. Sending up those satellites creates problems around us. It is dangerous times.

We are fencing ourselves in. We can't get out. The Shoshone are told we can't stay here on our homeland because the land belongs to someone else. U.S. tax dollars are creating this.

Those trees, "weeyum," or buck-berries, are disappearing, the main food we survived on. All the berries are drying up and all the roots that used to be here. We're wiping them out with our knowledge. It's creating bad things, killing Mother Earth.

The meat we eat—we give the cows something to grow faster. We create problems for that animal and problems for ourselves. It's a tough world that I see.

This year, more youngsters than ever are at the Test Site. It makes me feel real good about that. My prayer is not only for Native Peoples, but for everybody. We are all in the same boat. The Soviet Union had a power plant explosion. They lost many lives. They know that. And they will lose many more.

Yucca Mountain [site for the proposed U.S. Nuclear Waste Repository] lies asleep like a snake. When you walk on top of the mountain, it feels like you are walking on dried snakeskin. Someday, when we wake that snake up, a few of us will have to sit down and talk to that snake. It will get mad and rip open. When it awakens, we will all go to sleep. With his tail, that snake will move the mountain, rip it open, and the poison will come out on the surface. Long ago, the Indians talked about it. They see it is going to happen.

At Battle Mountain, before the white man and the trains, there was a vision among my people that a snakelike thing travelling over the land was coming, winding and smoking with fire to keep it rolling on rails of metal. A thousand years ago, our visions told of cars running on something soft—rubber. Smoke was coming out of them. Today, we see those things create problems for our sun, which will turn against us, and create problems for our skin. We don't have protection.

We must take care of the fire, and keep it clean, so it will take care of us. Our Mother Earth says the same thing. "Take care of me, and I will take care of you." This is the Law of the Land.

We Shoshone have not been keeping our traditions. We have drifted away from that. We had ceremonies for plants and living things.

At the Ceremony of the Seeds, we gathered every seed around throughout Shoshone country when it was ripe. We set a day in the fall of the year for the Ceremony of the Seeds. Our religious leader would pray—the winds would carry the seeds everywhere.

There is a season for everything, seeds above and below the ground. Fish—salmon used to migrate here. Berries. We used to hunt elk, deer, and buffalo. There were rabbits all year round, and birds and pine nuts. We followed their cycle with thanksgiving prayer, and cleansing before our ceremony.

Our secrets are sacred. We are instructed not to broadcast them. They are really not secret, but they are sacred. Our ancestors thousands of years ago passed this knowledge on from the Creator. Today, I tell you about it. I have to pass it on to somebody younger. Somebody has to guide the gifted people. If they are not guided by someone who understands, we are lost. Some of you out there are gifted, but very few. What you can do to help—spread the word about what you have learned here. Spread the word about the injustice here.

We can't get our own people together for the Ceremony of the Seeds. They don't understand anymore. So you, the gifted people, have to do it because everything out there is relying on us.

Photo: Linda Putnam

Direct action at the U.S. Dept. of Energy, Las Vegas, October 1992

Photo: Linda Putnam

Nevada-Semipalatinsk Movement, Nevada Test Site, January 1991
"Take care of the fire so that you can continue on . . ."

Comprehensive Test Ban:
    President Clinton's historic July 3, 1993 announcement that he would extend the U.S. nuclear testing moratorium until at least September 1994—unless another nation conducted a nuclear test—and pursue a comprehensive test ban (CTB) has received a positive international response, and makes it likely that the U.S. will never explode a nuclear test again.

    By reducing funding for the U.S. test site, Congress has reinforced the decision to extend the moratorium, even if another nation tests. With his decision, President Clinton has opted to put overall nuclear disarmament and nonproliferation goals ahead of the special interests of the U.S. nuclear weapons establishment. The positive international response provides an opportunity for multilateral agreement on a CTB treaty.

    Russia has taken the position that it will not be the first nation to resume nuclear testing. France is in favor of a complete test ban treaty, on the condition that it is universal and verifiable.

    A Chinese test would create a political dilemma for the leaders of other nuclear nations, and indeed, they conducted a test October 3, 1994, the very day Corbin sat in the Chinese embassy in Washington, D.C. urging them not to test. The Chinese ignored world opinion, because they said, the United States would not give up their "first-strike" position.
    Source: The 1993 Campaign for a Nuclear Test Ban. Physicians for Social Responsibility

Photo: Linda Putnam

Western Shoshone and Kazakh Peace Pipe Ceremony,
Nevada Test Site, January 1991

Russia:

It is my great honor to invite you to participate in the First Congress of the Global Anti-nuclear Alliance to be held in the Kazakhstan capital, Alma Ata, August 29 to September 2, 1993. The date of this Congress coincides with two dates: the first Soviet atomic bomb was tested at the main U.S.S.R. nuclear test site near Semipalatinsk on August 29, 1949, and this very test site was shut down officially on August 29, 1991, forty-two years later.

As a result of the People's Moratorium, implemented by the Nevada-Semipalatinsk non-governmental anti-nuclear movement, our main task is to discuss how we can achieve a world-wide comprehensive test ban, and to point out to the world community the medical and ecological consequences of nuclear weapons production and testing, and the impact of low-level radiation upon living things.

—from the invitation by
Olzhas Suleimenov, President of the
Nevada-Semipalatinsk Movement
(NSM), Alma-Ata

Photo: James Lerager

*Corbin and Olzhas Suleimenov, leader of the movement
to stop testing in Kazakhstan*

Semipalatinsk: A Place of
Weeping and a Place of Sorrow
by Cathie Lyons

   The orphanage opened in
1981. It is the major facility
caring for the children who bear
the most severe biological and
genetic aftereffects of the
region's nuclear testing. Many
of the children at Ayaguz are
mentally retarded. Some are
blind. Many have tumors. Most
have seizures. Some have limb
malformations. Many are
ambulatory, but some are not.
There are those with growth
retardation and with cerebral
palsy.
   In Alma-Ata, the capital of
Kazakhstan, the Minister of
Health refers to the Semipalatinsk region as "our place of
weeping and our place of
sorrow." This was the "unin-
habited" place chosen by Stalin
to be the Soviet Union's
Polygon (military test ground).
Here, from 1949 to 1989, the
earth trembled and the atmo-

sphere convulsed from the force of 563 nuclear explosions.

For years, what happened at Semipalatinsk and its effects on human health and the environment would be classified information. Even forty years later, the Kazakh people knew very little about the sustained effects of exposure to low-dose radiation. After citizen protesters were gunned down in 1989 in Alma-Ata, the people of Kazakhstan rose up and started a national anti-nuclear movement. Sick at heart over what the inhabitants of the Semipalatinsk region had been forced to endure, the Kazakhs converged on Alma-Ata demanding an end to all nuclear testing—not only there, but by all nations.

In his *Memoirs*, Andrei Sakharov recounts the H-bomb test: "The customary mushroom cloud gradually formed. . . . We drove in open cars past buildings destroyed by the blast, braking to a stop beside an eagle whose wings had been badly singed. . . . I have been told that thousands of birds are destroyed during every test. They take wing at the flash but then fall to earth, burned and blinded."

Bakhyt Tumenova, a medical doctor, has responsibility to oversee public health in the aftermath of forty years of nuclear testing. "During spot checks, we have found high rates of sickness among our children and high rates of oncological diseases. Almost ninety percent of women suffer from anemia in the districts adjacent to the test site. These women are young . . . and they are ill. Year after year, the number of miscarriages and stillbirths goes up. We have a high rate of children with birth defects and congenital malformations. Almost half of our population exhibits immunodeficiency. Many people are found with chromosome changes and chromosome aberrations. This is only part of the information that shows the grave consequences of nuclear testing."

In the words of Dr. Tumenova: "All of the people of our region live a similar destiny. It has affected us and it will affect our children and their children. We know from Japanese scientists that the most serious genetic malformations will occur in the third and fourth generations—the generations of our children and our grandchildren. Come here, see it with your own eyes. Nuclear testing does not choose to affect people according to their race, national origin, or sex. This terrible experiment that was carried out in our region in Kazakhstan is a crime not only against our own people but against all of humanity."

Source: *New World Outlook*, March-April 1994

Call to Action

As Native people, we're not looking to support ourselves alone, because I think many people throughout the world are already concerned with this nuclear enemy. Soon, everyone is going to be saying that we're going to have to put a stop to all this.

I would like to see people start talking to other people, getting together, and asking questions such as: What are we going to do? Who shall do it? Who wants to talk about what? How can we get together? What can we say to each other? Let's not be ashamed or shy. I used to be ashamed, but here I am, speaking up.

Let's not have a sickly world out there. Don't abuse, don't overuse what we have in resources out there, such as oil and gas, coal, and different things. Use them sparingly. Even electricity, we need to use it sparingly.

Support your Indian nations, your Native peoples, throughout the world, because it's been given to the Native people everywhere to take care of this world. Go out and do something for the Indian people, who are suffering today, as I see it, throughout the world, not only in California, Nevada, Idaho, but in every other place. We continue to suffer because nobody has been listening to us, and all along they have taken our land away from us and used it to destroy the rest of the world.

I hope people will really think about this and write letters and so on to your Congressmen, and your leaders in Washington, D.C., to let them know your concern.

And the Indian people—we need to work together and talk together. Our elders used to work together, talk together, sing together, and so forth. We haven't been doing this, and we need

Photo: Linda Putnam

Thomas Banyacya at Nevada Test Site
calling for a new world of peace.

to, so that we can start coming out from behind the bush, and recognize that we are the caretakers of this Mother Earth.

At the Nevada Test Site, the Livermore Lab in California, and wherever we work, we have Morning Circle ceremonies every morning, and I remind the people of what we should be doing together—that it's very important to pray for our Mother Earth, so that she will continue to give us clean water and clean air and to provide something for the younger generation. And I tell them, "If we were following the spiritual way of life, we would never be doing what we're doing today—abusing our Mother Earth—because the spiritual way of life is to take care of what we've got."

I don't see any other way we can change the world, except by the people coming together, praying for the Earth, and then waking up the rest of us. A long time ago, the elders said that there would come a time when the Native people would have to lead everyone else out of this mess, so that's what we're trying to do now.

Photo: Hawkeye Haven

Photo: Paul John Miller/Black Star

Photo: Paul John Miller/Black Star

Joining Hands Together

We have to start joining together to pray. We all have to try to keep our Mother Earth clean. We are going to have to join hands together the best way we can and do one thing: pray.

There is a sickness among us today, and it is very sad to see these things: the earth, air, and water are becoming more and more contaminated, and people throughout the country are coming down with some kind of sickness. They don't know what it is, but it's taking a lot of their lives. One reason is that the government has knowingly used all of us as guinea pigs, and whenever we protest or go to court, we can never win because they make the rules.

I've been asking people everywhere I go to join in with the Indian people, because the Indian people are struggling, really struggling. You white people are the ones who can help join the Indian people together. And it's a fact: the white people in government listen to other white people protesting something, but if it's an Indian, they just want to take our picture with them and then send us away.

Photo: Paul John Miller/Black Star

Photo: Paul John Miller/Black Star

Photo: Paul John Miller/Black Star

Today we Indians are jealous of one another, and I don't know why—but now we don't have anywhere else to go. We've only got one Mother Earth, and we all need to work together. I think the Indian people have to be told that, as an Indian people, our job is to go out there and start doing it! I think this is why our spiritual leaders throughout the country are so divided. We don't want to see other spiritual people coming in and leading. For example, take me, coming into California. When I'm in California, it seems to me that some others are saying, "Why are you coming into my country? This is my problem. Your problem is over there; you should be over there doing what you can."

October 18, 1993

President Bill Clinton
The White House
Washington, D.C.

Dear Mr. President,
    I was in Washington for a week at the beginning of October, and I am
sorry that I could not meet with you personally, "the White Chief," about
the serious effects of nuclear testing and the radiation that is destroying our
Mother Earth.
    Coming to Washington was an important part of my work to stop
nuclear testing. I met with a number of government officials—with congress-
men and senators, officials from the Department of Energy regarding cleanup
of the test site in Nevada, peace groups, people against plutonium prolifera-
tion, and also a talk with the Chinese ambassador . . . on the morning of
October 4, the same day they exploded their bomb.
    As spiritual leader of the Western Shoshone nation, I want you to
understand how nuclear testing and nuclear waste affects not only our people
on native lands, but all living things on the earth.
    The whole world is quickly becoming contaminated. As I see it, time is
very short, and everything on the planet today is suffering. The water, air,
and Mother Earth herself is beginning to die from the effects of nuclear
power. What good will our world be in a few years if we are all suffering from
the effects of nuclear radiation?
    I have travelled to Kazakhstan and witnessed some very sad things. They
cannot use their water any more due to contamination. A few years ago, the
water spoke to me: "I'm going to look like water, but pretty soon no one is
going to be able to use me." You may not realize it, but time is running out
for the rest of us, too—all over the world.
    I have seen the effects of nuclear radiation, both in our country among
the "down-winders" and in Kazakhstan: children being born with eyes over
their ears, arms coming out of their sides, and many other birth defects, as
well as leukemia and cancers among the adults after only a short time.
    As human beings, we have broken our connection with our Mother
Earth. All the food that our people have relied upon for thousands of years is
beginning to die out. The berries and native plants are gone; the plants don't
grow strong like they used to; and the water is becoming contaminated all
over the planet. Even our traditional medicine plants are not growing as they
should, and are disappearing.

Our native ceremonies recognize our connection to the earth. We know that everything out there—all the living things: the trees, the plants, even the rocks—everything is conscious. Our Mother Earth is a living, conscious being. When all the people of the world realize this—that all living things need and use the same water, the same air—then we can begin to change our relationship to the earth. We have to bring this consciousness back to the people, and lead the people back to nature.

A long time ago our ancestors told us that some day the people would look to the Indian to lead us in the right direction. We came to Washington to work together with the people that run the government, because we are all in this mess together. I am not a scientist or nuclear physicist, nor can I solve the technical and very complex problem of how to deal with nuclear contamination.

I do know that we have to unite all the people of the earth, begin an honest dialogue of what has happened already, and work together to help save the earth. The earth is not an object for us to manipulate, but a living being that gives all of us life.

We pray to protect the land, and all living things out there. The spirit of the land has said to me that we're going to have to help her out. If we don't protect the land, our Mother Earth is going to suffer even more in the very near future.

We know that all people, no matter where they live, are natives of Mother Earth. We only have one water and one air that we all drink and breathe. You can help all of us by deciding not to contaminate the earth any further. We encourage you, Mr. President, to stand up and be strong in your decision to protect the earth.

Your decision not to continue testing—despite what the Chinese or French might do, and despite British urgings—will send a strong message to the other countries who are not so wise or conscious. Remember that this pollution and contamination is already spreading all over the earth, and our water is becoming radioactive.

I am speaking to you for all the people of the earth, and for all living things. I hope you will listen to me very carefully, take into your heart what I am saying, and then take all the right actions to help save our Mother Earth.

Sincerely,
Corbin Harney
Spiritual Leader of the Western Shoshone Nation

Talk in
the White House,
October 1994
Corbin Harney

Photo: Paul John Miller/Black Star

"I think it's very important for you people here today to really understand where the native people are coming from, because they were here when the white man came. We were discovered, as we understand today, through your people. Today, we are one people. I'm going to talk about all of us, we, the people today.

"The testing of nuclear bombs in my part of the country in Nevada is going to shorten our lives, you and I. We are going to be very sick people. We've begun to see that throughout the country today, not only here but throughout the world. The bomb that they have tested on our Shoshone land, near Las Vegas, is very dangerous to me and to you. The children behind you are the ones who are going to suffer the most.

"Today all the living things on this planet that we're on have begun to suffer. We all know that all the living things are beginning to die. What are we doing about it? So far I see a lot on the surface, lots of beautiful talk, and so forth. We, the people, are going to have to stand up and say 'no' to nuclear energy. We talk about how cheap it is, how good

it is. This life we see up here is really beautiful. But, you know, it's going to shorten your life.

"Those are the things Indian people have talked about for thousands of years. We cannot have lip service and continue to be told a lie. We've been lied to for six hundred years. Today let's change that so we'll have cleaner water to drink, not only for the humans, but for all the living things on this earth that we are on today.

"Everything uses water, I don't care what it is uses water. This building we are standing in today uses water. The house we have today uses water. Water gives everything strength on this mother earth. The air that we breathe today has begun to be contaminated with all kinds of chemicals—and radiation.

"We don't realize we are causing all the bad things on this earth. This earth needs our support; this is the

Photo: Paul John Miller/Black Star

mommy that we cannot live without. We only have one mother here, trying its best to feed us, but we are still sucking our mother dry, which should never happen, but we still let it continue to happen.

"I hope that we do unite as one people around the world, that we have a cleaner life for the younger generation, the tree life, the plant life, the animal life, the bird life, the rock life we use for healing our sick. Today the Spirit in all of those things I talk about has begun to die. We know that. We talk about it, the scientists talk about it; we know that. Today some places, in the 'big water' as I call it, we have fishes dying; you know that as well as I do. Your crab is dying by the millions down the coast of Washington and

Oregon. I know because I was there.

"Today you, as the people, can change direction. We have to have unity among us. We cannot say, let somebody else do it. Each and every one of you people can unite yourselves together. Let's have one voice, one ear, not two or three of them. We've heard a forked tongue for many a years. Let's not have that forked tongue any more.

"I hope you will carry this message on around the globe, because we've only got one water, one air, one Mother Earth that we are all on. We all use those three things. I hope the white chief here in this part of the country will really understand, and have the strength to support the Indian nations throughout the world. Thank you."

Photo: Paul John Miller/Black Star

Photo: Paul John Miller/Black Star

Washington, D.C., October 1994

Photo: Paul John Miller/Black Star

But I've been trying to spread the word that we're all involved in it—all the spiritual people; we are all involved in one thing—and that's to stop this nuclear testing throughout the world before it takes our life. That's something that we as an Indian people talked about long ago, and now we have to start uniting our people the best way we can.

I go out to my country and see what's taking place there. I have seen that my food, the wild food that my people survive on—the pine nuts, the chokecherries, and a lot of things—is disappearing; those foods are not growing there any more. If they are there, then they are contaminated. How can we survive on contaminated food? I've been saying these things now for the last few years. We have to join hands together, and there are no two ways about it.

My concern is for the young people—how will they survive? They need to know that they can survive. I've been fighting to save what we can, fighting the people who want to ban our religious sites, our spiritual ground, and our burial sites. I've been fighting for those issues over the last few years, not only in California, Nevada, and Idaho, but all throughout the country.

This is what I'm saying to people: I'm asking the white people, or whatever color you are, to go out there, but step back a little bit to give a chance to the Indian people, to let them do their thing. I'm also saying, don't get in front of the Indian people and say, "I this and I that," because that "I" is not going to work. This gets into the jealous part that I'm talking about. When we say "I," everybody gets tight and says, "Well, if he wants to do something, let him do it," and so the Indians walk away from it. And so I think that "I" is not the way.

Only *together* can we do something, but it is very hard for Indian people to trust the whites, because right from the beginning when the white man asked the Indian people what they knew about different things, our story came out in their books. But all the stories that I have seen so far in any book—I don't care what book it is—never was the truth; it always had something in it to say the white man was good and the Indian was a savage. So now we've got to get away from that in order to join together to do what we need to do.

I hope we can get together to pray for our Mother Earth. I hope everybody can do that. I never have changed my message. I had a vision that somewhere, sometime, we are going to be united together as a people to have a cleaner life than what we're coming through so far, but it's going to take maybe thirty or forty more years; that's the message that I've gotten so far.

For the past few years, we've called all the Native people together to come out to Rock Creek canyon, to have our voices heard there. And now people are really beginning to come out and talk about these things that are affecting our life all over the country. These are poor people doing it, not the rich people. The poorer we are, the more concerned we are. My people today, the Native people walking this Mother Earth with nothing in their pockets, they're struggling, but people seem to refuse to believe that they are struggling, and nobody seems to want to listen.

Only now are we beginning to get help. Everybody is putting their hand into what we're trying to do, and I think that is very, very good. I'm not one of those guys who's a good speaker, but I'm doing the best that I can. I think that other spiritual people have been told through the spirits out there, that "You people are going to have to start getting together and start doing your thing; in order to have the spiritual way of life, we're going to have to start bringing the people together."

Somewhere there has to be a center set up from which we can work, but I'm still searching for where that place can be. We can start to put down roots from that center. The spiritual people are going to have to get together from there. They're the ones who are going to have to lead us in the right direction.

Then we'll start talking about how we're going to bring the rain down to the places where it's dry, in all the places where we haven't been taking care of things, what kind of moisture we want, what kind of berries we want out there, what kind of herbs we're going to have, and how we're going to survive from them.

We're going to have to do away with the chemical stuff that we're doing today. We are all suffering from that, but we don't realize it. As spiritual people, we are going to have to clear those things away. One way to start doing it is through sweat. Sweat clears your body. It clears your mind. You pray for each other. You don't single somebody out. We're all the same, one humanity.

Corbin in Sweden:
   "I came thousands and thousands of miles to be here with you. I thought that by doing this, we can start working together as a people to put a stop to nuclear testing over the world so that we can have a cleaner life, clean world, clean water, clean air. I hope that we do work together, because you young people are going to have to rely on us, and the unborn have to rely on us. We are the ones who can do it.

   "We're fighting something that we don't understand. But even though nuclear power is very dangerous, they're still using it today. I hope sometime soon we can put an end, a stop to it."

Stephan Dompke, Director, Society for a Nuclear Free Future, Berlin:
   "Indigenous peoples and cultures have a spiritual foundation which is precisely what we lack in Western civilization. That's why I think people like Corbin will be of tremendous importance, and you can see it in this conference (Sweden). He gives another quality, a totally new quality to what we are doing. He provides strength. When we go home, we will remember people like Corbin as a living example of determination and a true spiritual strength. You can see that he is a very humorous person and is never in a bad mood ever.

   "He addresses fundamental questions that we tend to forget about because we live in an artificial world. I think it's a true sign of spirituality to be able to laugh about yourself. That type of humor to me is a sign of true spirituality. To open one's heart is the fundamental thing, then comes knowledge. But you have to have the open heart, and Corbin opens your heart. He took up a burden and he assumes the responsibility and carries the burden for the whole world.

   "There will be no peace in the outside world if there is no peace in yourself. Corbin is truly a person who has that peace in himself. He is that living example, and there are very few people around who express that peace and strength the way he does."

We have to start taking care of our Mother Earth, all of us, throughout the world, and not only here. We figure it's good in another country, in Russia, for instance, that they're better off than we are, but they're not; they're suffering over there, and we're suffering here.

Some of us, like Claudia Peterson, Bill Rosse, and myself, have been abroad to England, Germany, Sweden, and Russia, and have tried to get support from people overseas. They are supporting us all the way, because they are going through the same thing.

Lesson from Stockholm

Some of us were invited in 1990 to travel to Stockholm, Sweden, to attend the convention of the International Physicians for the Prevention of Nuclear War. We were there to organize another organization, the Global Anti-Nuclear Alliance (GANA). It is made up of people around the globe coming together to start preserving the Mother Earth and to stop the testing and the development of nuclear energy.

When I walked around the city of Stockholm, which is over seven hundred years old, I saw a message that was laid there in the way the buildings and streets were built. They were done by spiritual people who were there before, and I think that's why the city is today a beautiful place. Things are laid according to the contour of the ground and so on. It has a good feeling, and continues to give a good feeling to the people and everything else.

The brick pattern in the streets was laid by a spiritual person. It had to be, the way it's laid. It's been there for hundreds

Corbin and Bill Rosse, Sr.

In Stockholm:

"I feel good that we came and have been able to talk to the Swedish people and that we understand each other. Like I said, you've got the same water as I've got over there. You've got the same air we breathe, because if it were different, I wouldn't drink your water and you wouldn't drink my water, and so forth. So we've got one water. We know we've got one air. We've got one planet out here that grows all our food for us. I think those are the things we're going to have to bring out to the younger generation today."

of years and it will never wash away, because it's laid according to the contour of the ground, the way the soil lays. It's put there in such a way that it will last. I'm proud of what they did. You don't see this in the so-called New World, our part of the world.

The street is patterned for the water. The people here who made that design had their spirit with the water. All the bricks are laid according to the way the ground slants, with a curved design. The water has something to do with the design, because of the way it flows. The people who laid it there understood that they were working with nature, with the spirit of the water, and the way it flows. They knew exactly what damage that water could cause. Very spiritual people came up with that design.

Now, people today, they walk on it, they drive on it, and they don't even hurt the design that was put there. Water can't wash it away and won't wash the ground away because of the way the design is laid. The bricks separate the flows of water from each other, in other words, so it flows freely, and still at the same time, it doesn't damage the rocks that were put there.

It's just like the beaver would build a dam. When the dam is built by the beaver, you can't wash it away. The beaver, we know, has a spiritual way of life, and the same with the people who built those streets in the city of Stockholm. The streets are still there, because of their design. Their forefathers here were pretty smart! It's something that we can learn from today.

It gave me hope that two people, from across different sides of the pond, can unite as one people, because we're under one Creator. One Creator put us here, divided with water. I could hear the water singing there in Stockholm, singing with its voice. Every once in a while I could hear it, and the songs that I used to sing, I heard there in the water.

Peace

It's so important for us to have peace. The fire has peace, the air has peace, the Mother Earth is peaceful; all the elements are trying their best to continue to support what's growing on this Earth. Whatever's here is supporting us in a peaceful way, but we're not doing the same in return. We're not doing things in a peaceful way to all the living things out there. It's why we have to unite ourselves together in peace.

Peace is very important. We have to live in as peaceful a way as we can. Truth is something really hard to come by. We all know that something bad can happen so fast, so quick that we don't realize it's happening. But something good comes slowly and takes a very long time to build up. All the people who join together in prayer, or who come out to the Test Site and to the other gatherings, they are trying to bring about change in as peaceful a way as they can.

Message to Young People

*"We see that Corbin's work helps to bring these
kids away from the alcohol and drugs that are so
destructive, and that it also brings them to the
point where they become healthy young adults,
future leaders of the tribes, and eventually the
elders who will carry on."*
                    —Pat Knight, Elko, Nevada

Put This in Your Hearts

I f we had followed the spiritual way of life, we would never
have been doing what we're doing today, because the spiritual way of life is to take care of what we've got, so that we
can have a cleaner life and continue to live on.

The reason we haven't been doing what our forefathers
practiced for thousands of years is that we thought our life was
too hard that way. Today we're beginning to realize that we have
to connect with the spirits out there in order for us to continue.

I have been trying to practice this and to show you, our
young people, what we should be doing. I ask you young people
to put this into your hearts, to learn from it, and to do your thing,
so that way we'll have a cleaner life for the younger generation.

We have gifted youngsters out there, but they're ashamed.
We're shameful people to begin with. I'm concerned about you
youngsters, about what kind of life you are going to go through,
and your kids on down—what they are going to do, how they are

Photo: Nancy Clemens

"Some of you youngsters are going to be our leaders;
you are the ones we are going to have to depend on."

going to survive. It's very important to think about those things now.

Some of you youngsters are going to be our leaders; you are the ones we are going to have to depend on. All the living things out here have to depend on you, because we were put here to take care of this Mother Earth. We have to get together, like our forefathers did, to bring moisture of some kind where the land is parched and dried out. You and I have to ask for rain to come down, so that the grass will continue to grow again.

Somehow we have to be connected back to things in order to hear the rain, the plants, and whatever, telling us what to do, how to go about setting things right. The Creator, the Spirit that's in those things, is looking at us now, but never saying anything. Our gifted people are not saying anything either. Our leaders, who are supposed to be spiritual leaders, who are connected to the tree life, plant life, and so on, they haven't been saying anything.

Our people have been hiding behind a lot of lies, alcohol, and nowadays that marijuana smoke that they smoke. When people go that way, their mind disappears—it's not there any more. If we continue to do that, where are we going to be? Where are all the youngsters going to be within another ten to twenty years, if that's the kind of life we have to live?

We know these things are poison. We humans are the only beings who don't seem to understand how poisonous these things are. The animals, the birds, they understand. They know that if a horse eats a poison weed, he'll never eat it again, but we continue on and on, taking poison, until we ruin our life or take our own life. This is exactly where we're headed.

That's not the way we should be. We should be clean people. We should be really knowledgeable about what's going on out there. Our elders got away from us. They told us, "Hey, you guys are living too fast; you're telling us we're too old," and so on.

You, our youngsters, are going to be our leaders. I keep saying, some of you are going to lead us. You are going to have to lead your generation. Now is the time for you youngsters to really think about things. Ask your parents, or ask your grand-parents. Make sure whether what I say and what I teach is the

"My kids have deep respect for Corbin. They really like him and like teasing with him. He has this way with the kids . . . he would probably just spend all day with them and the kids would never get bored. He just has this fascinating personality. I think it makes them realize that they've lost a strong heritage and now, seeing Corbin, my kids have come back to me and said, 'So this is what you've been telling us all this time.'"

—Irene Moon

right thing, because in my time, this is the way things were done.

We are tied to what's out there. We're connected to it, all the tree life, everything, even though we might not realize it. Everybody is connected to every tree. If we weren't connected, the trees wouldn't be eating and they wouldn't be breathing air like we do. Trees breathe air. They eat and so on. They have to be talked to.

Some people grow plants in their houses. They sing songs to them, talk to them, and so on, and they grow better. This shows how you are connected to things. It's very important to learn something about our spiritual ways. Ask your grandparents; they'll tell you the same thing as what I say. However, they might not say anything the first time you ask them. You have to keep asking them. After a while, if you keep asking them, they'll start telling you about those things—the stories that were told by our people, our history.

But it's not just a story, like those coyote stories, or the wolf and coyote story—they really happened. At one time, all the living things here talked. At one time they had voices, and they moved like we do. They're still moving, but we came afterwards when they became plant life, and this is where we're headed. We're going to be plant life! You come from the earth, and you're going to go back into it.

We have to remember that all living things on this earth have spirits. Some of us talk to the Spirit in things. Others don't even realize that there's a Spirit out there, but there is. Some of you young people have heard the voice of the Spirit now and then. If you hear something out there, that's the Spirit. It's very important to learn how to recognize these things.

Make Offerings

Always offer something to what you get off the land. Bless what you get off the Mother Earth.

Bless the water. Talk to it, keep it alive, keep it moving. Keep the Spirit in the water moving. If you talk to it and bless it, it really keeps the water happy, gives it strength.

Good Things Take Work

There are two things that are very important to all people, whether they're ninety or a hundred years old, or one day old. Bad things come easily, very easily. You can get mad easily. You can say things easily, you can tell lies easily, and so on.

Good things come hard, awfully hard. It's so easy to tell lies and do the wrong things. Doing a good thing is harder—you have to work hard at it. You yourself have to think very strongly about these two things: what is hard and what is easy. When you are young is the time to think about it.

Make a good life for yourself, and don't do the wrong thing. Wrong is something that will be easy to come by. A good thing is going to be harder to get to. You are young. You have to make a good life for yourself, and it will be hard to come by. You have to struggle down the road. To do bad things, you don't have to struggle at all; they're very easy to do.

Photo: Dan True

Corbin:

"There are hummingbirds always connected to me for some reason, I don't know why. Wherever I go, the hummingbirds are watching over me . . . I always see them flying around. Not too long ago, we were having ceremonies and a spiritual gathering, and this hummingbird came and landed on my shoulder. There were a couple of Hopis there, like Thomas Banyacya, and when he saw that, he thought, by God, I must be something. It was pretty hard to believe, because the hummingbird is connected to God in their way. When he saw that, he just couldn't believe it. But I've always liked those little birds from the beginning of my life. They can fly backwards and forwards.

"We've got our doubts about a lot of things, but we know the Spirit is up there trying to work with us. But something is always holding us back. Those are the reasons why I always say, there's two things here, the good thing and the bad thing. A bad thing will always take over the good thing. It takes a long time for a good thing to happen; it takes one step at a time. But a bad thing can happen real fast. That's why we've got to trust in that Spirit, and trust in ourselves that we'll know the right thing to do when the time comes."

I'm telling you to do the good things, even if it's going to be hard and you have to struggle to get there. Only after you pass a certain point in time, then you'll begin to realize and understand what I'm saying.

When you're young, it doesn't go far into your ear, but remember this: a good thing comes a step at a time. Bad things happen so fast that you don't realize they've happened. The tongue can say a bad thing in just a second. But a good thing takes thought and time—you have to think about what you're going to say and so on. A good thing is something that feels good or makes a person feel good.

Ask Your Grandparents

Young people don't often understand what this life is all about. They think that what the older people say is just a story that somebody dreamed up. But once we lose that connection between the Spirit world and us, then who can we rely on?

Ask your grandparents—they are the ones we learn from. We have to rely on the older people, just like the animals all rely on their mommies. Our mommies show us how. All of us have seen ducks going down the road; wherever they go, the mommy leads them. Even the tiniest creatures on the land have a mommy that they follow around. When you find little things with their mommies, you should leave them alone, because they are living in their home, and they need to survive here too.

The mommy teaches the little one how to survive. We humans have gotten away from these understandings. We Indians are not trying to pick up a piece of paper to learn from, or read a book to try and see where the beginning of life is. My fore-

Florence Vega and Eunice Silva

Eunice Silva, Western Shoshone Medicine Woman, over 100 years old: *"When my Mama took me to the white people's church, I said, 'Mama, no, I don't want to do like that. I have my own way. I do not understand that book. How can all the living things hear the prayers from inside a box?' I do my Indian way. I go outside to pray. I pray to Mother Earth and Father Earth for everything. That's how I do."*

Corbin and Mike Clemens

"You young people are going to become our future leaders. Take care of what you've got in order to live on."

Photo: Christina Clemens

fathers told me that a piece of paper doesn't mean anything, because you can keep changing the words on the piece of paper.

Our way can never be changed. Our forefathers wrote something on a piece of rock; you can never change it. Nowadays we don't even know how to read the writing on the rocks, because we didn't listen to our parents and grandparents when they talked about it. Now we have to try and get somebody else to read it to us, even though it's something we should all know about and understand. You youngsters are the ones we are going to rely on. You'll have to pick all this up and start telling your youngsters all about it.

Sometimes I'm just lost about the whole thing. I don't know where to start or how to go about it. I wish I did, but I don't. We are trying to do something for our people, but we have lost our ways. We got away from our Sun Dance, for instance. Now in Germany the white man is doing a Sun Dance, even though they've changed it a lot, and we have to learn from them what we're already supposed to know!

On paper, they have books all about the Indian ways and the things we used to do, all written up on paper. We, the people who are supposed to know all about it, are in total darkness. Very few of us even talk our native tongue any more. It gives me a great hope for the future when I hear a young person say they are going to go back home and start learning their native tongue. They might not be able to ask their parents, because their parents may not know either, but they should continue to ask people until they find someone who can teach them.

Take Care of Mommy

Your life begins with mommy. Mommy is very important to us and all the living things here. Mommy is very important to the trees. They had to have mommy in order for them to survive, to learn how to live, and to learn how to continue their life. Our mommy began from the Mother Earth, and just as everything alive has to have mommy, we have to have mommy in order to live on. So it's very important to take care of our mommy.

Everything I talk about has to have mommy—all the plant life, the little animal life, the little creatures—all have mommies. So it's very important for you youngsters to continue to take care of what you've got.

My people used to say, "Even if it's nothing, take care of it; somewhere it's going to turn into something worthwhile to live for." Some of us came through a rough life, not everyone, but we each have a life that we've got to take care of. No one else is going to live your life. You have to live your life: you are the one. It's your life, and it's very important that you make that one life as good as you can. Make the best of your life.

Some of us are showing you youngsters what life is about. If you want to understand the tree life, the animal life, the bird life, you have to think about them, about what kind of life they've come through. In order to be here, some of the birds have had to suffer just to live. Some of the animal life has to suffer. When we take the time to go out and be with them, they're happy to see us; we're happy to see them.

This is why I always repeat, "Take care of them." They like to live their life, just like we do. They want to live on. Even a little ant likes to live on. They don't want to be disturbed; they don't want to end their life.

Life is important to us all.

Continue Our Prayers and Ceremonies

It's very important to do the ceremonies and prayers; that's why I do them for people, for you youngsters. I'd like to see young people do what I'm doing back in their own home parts, so that we have a beginning. For example, in some places they do start their council meetings with prayers first.

The important part of all the get-togethers is praying together. Ask a lot of questions about it; it's the only way to learn. I just tell what I've learned from my older people, what they told me: *take care of what you've got in order to live on.*

It's very important for all of us to get together again and again. Wherever there is a gathering, I like to be invited, and I get

"Don't be afraid to ask a lot of questions.
This is how I learned, by asking questions."

to as many as I can. When they are far apart, it gets hard sometimes, but I do my best. I'm trying to pass my knowledge on to the younger people so that you all can carry it on, maybe better than I do.

I'm trying to take care of what we've got. I'm concerned about you young people, what kind of life you're going to go through, and your kids on down, what they'll be doing, how they're going to survive.

Some of you go to church and pray together. That is very important, and it's what we must do. We have to pray to the sun, the earth, the water, and to the air. I hope that we will all pick up this message that I'm putting out, so that we can have a cleaner life, and so the younger generation can continue on.

Appendices

Treaty of Ruby Valley, 1863

Treaty between the United States of America and the Western Bands of Shoshone Indians. Concluded October 1, 1863; Ratification advised with amendment, June 26, 1866; Amendment assented to June 17, 1869; Proclaimed October 21, 1969.

ULYSSES S. GRANT, PRESIDENT OF THE UNITED STATES OF AMERICA, TO ALL AND SINGULAR TO WHOM THESE PRESENTS SHALL COME, GREETING:

Whereas a Treaty was made and concluded at Ruby Valley, in the Territory of Nevada, on the first day of October, in the year of our Lord one thousand eight hundred and sixty-three, by and between James W. Nye and James Duane Doty, Commissioners, on the part of the United States, and Te-moak, Mo-ho-a, Kirk-weedgwa, To-nag, and other Chiefs, Principal Men, and Warriors of the Western Bands of the Shoshonee Nation of Indians, on the part of said bands of Indians, and duly authorized thereto by them, which Treaty is in the words and figures following to wit:

Treaty of Peace and Friendship made at Ruby Valley, in the Territory of Nevada, this first day of October, A.D. one thousand eight hundred and sixty-three, between the United States of America, represented by the undersigned Commissioners, and the Western Bands of the Shoshonee Nation of Indians, represented by their Chiefs and Principal Men and Warriors, as follows:

ARTICLE I.

Peace and friendship shall be hereafter established and maintained between the Western Bands of the Shoshonee nation and the people and Government of the United States; and the said bands stipulate and agree that hostilities and all depredations upon the emigrant trains, the mail and telegraph lines, and upon the citizens of the United States within their country, shall cease.

ARTICLE II.

The several routes of travel through the Shoshonee country, now or hereafter used by white men, shall be forever free, and unobstructed by the said bands, for the use of the government of the United States, and of all emigrants and travelers under its authority and protection, without molestation or injury from them. And if depredations are at any time committed by bad men of their nation, the offenders shall be immediately taken and delivered up to the proper officers of the United States, to be punished as their offences shall deserve; and the safety of all travellers passing peaceably over either said routes is hereby guarantied by said bands.

Military posts may be established by the President of the United States along said routes or elsewhere in their country; and station houses may be erected and occupied at such points as may be necessary for the comfort and convenience of travellers or for the mail or telegraph companies.

ARTICLE III.

The telegraph and overland stage lines having been established and operated by companies under the authority of the United States through a part of the Shoshonee country, it is expressly agreed that the same may be continued without hindrance, molestation, or injury from the people of said bands, and that their property and the lives and property of passengers in the stages and of the employees of the respective companies, shall be protected by them. And further, it being understood that provision has been made by the government of the United States for the construction of a railway from the plains west to the Pacific ocean, it is stipulated by said bands that the said railway or its branches may be located, constructed, and operated, and without molestation from them, through any portion of country claimed or occupied by them.

ARTICLE IV.

It is further agreed by the parties hereto, that the Shoshonee country may be explored and prospected for gold and silver, or other minerals; and when mines are discovered, they may be worked, and mining and agricultural settlements formed, and ranches established whenever they may be required. Mills may be erected and timber taken for their use, as also for building or other purposes in any part of the country claimed by said bands.

ARTICLE V.

It is understood that the boundaries of the country claimed and occupied by said bands are defined and described by them as follows:

On the north by Wong-gogo-da Mountains and Shoshonee River Valley; on the west by Su-non-to-yah Mountains or Smith Creek Mountains; on the south by Wi-co-bah and the Colorado Desert; on the east by Po-ho-no-be Valley or Steptoe Valley and Great Salt Lake Valley.

ARTICLE VI.

The said bands agree that whenever the President of the United States shall deem it expedient for them to abandon the roaming life, which they now lead, and become herdsmen or agriculturalists, he is hereby authorized to make such reservations for their use as he may deem necessary within the country above described; and they do also hereby agree to remove their camps to such reservations as he may indicate, and to reside and remain therein.

ARTICLE VII.

The United States, being aware of the inconvenience resulting to the Indians in consequence of the driving away and destruction of game along the routes travelled by white men, and by the formation of agricultural and mining settlements, are willing to fairly compensate them for the same, therefore, and in consideration of the proceeding stipulations, and of their faithful observance by the said bands, the United States promise and agree to pay to the said bands of the Shoshonee nation parties hereto, annually for the term of twenty years, the sum of five thousand dollars in such articles, including cattle for herding or other purposes, as the President of the United States shall deem suitable for their wants and condition, either as hunters or herdsmen. And the said bands hereby acknowledge the reception of the said stipulated annuities as a full compensation and equivalent for the loss of game and the rights and privileges hereby conceded.

ARTICLE VIII.

The said bands hereby acknowledge that they have received from said commissioners provisions and clothing amounting to thousand dollars as presents at the conclusion of this treaty.

Done at Ruby Valley the day and year above written.

JAMES W. NYE	KIRK-WEEDGWA
JAMES DUANE DOTY	TO-NAG
TE-MOAK	TO-SO-WEE-SO-OP
MO-HO-A	SOW-ER-E-GAH

```
    PO-ON-GO-SAH              KO-RO-KOAT-ZE
    PAR-A-WOAT-ZE             PON-GE-MAH
    GA-HA-DIER               BUCK
```
Witnesses:
J.B. MOORE, Lt. Col. 3rd INf, Cal. Vol.
JACOB T. LOCKHART,
    Indian Agent Nev. Ter.
HENRY BUTTERFIELD, Interpreter

And whereas, the said Treaty having been submitted to the Senate of the United States for its constitutional action thereon, the Senate did, on the twenty-sixth day of June, one thousand eight hundred and sixty-six, advise and consent to the ratification of the same, with an amendment, by a resolution in the words and figures following, to wit:

IN EXECUTIVE SESSION,
SENATE OF THE UNITED STATES,

June 26, 1866.

Resolved, (two-thirds of the Senators present concurring,) That the Senate advise and consent to the ratification of the Treaty of peace and friendship made at Ruby Valley, in the Territory of Nevada, the first day of October, A.D. one thousand eight hundred and sixty-three, between the United States of America, represented by their Commissioners, and the Western Bands of the Shoshonee Nation of Indians, represented by their Chiefs and Principal Men and Warriors, with the following
AMENDMENT:
Fill the blank in the 8th article with the word five.
Attest:

J.W. FORNEY,
Secretary

And whereas, the foregoing amendment having been fully explained and interpreted to the undersigned Chiefs, Principal Men, and Warriors of the Western Bands of the Shoshonee Nation of Indians, they did, on the seventeenth day of June, one thousand eight hundred and sixty-nine, give their free and voluntary assent to the said amendment, in the words and figures following, to wit:

Whereas the Senate of the United States, in executive session, did advise and consent to the ratification of the Treaty of peace and friendship, made at Ruby Valley, in the Territory of Nevada, on the first day of October, one thousand eight hundred and sixty-three, by the Commissioners on the part of the United States and the Western

Bands of the Shoshonee Nation of Indians, represented by their Chiefs
and Principal Men and Warriors, with the following amendment:

"Fill the blank in the 8th article with the word five."

And whereas the foregoing amendment has been fully interpreted
and explained to the undersigned Chiefs and Principal Men and Warriors of the aforesaid Western Bands of the Shoshonee Nation of
Indians, we do hereby agree and assent to the same.

Done at Ruby Valley, Nevada, on this 17th day of June, A.D. 1869.
Attest:

J.H. DAWLEY	TIM-OOK
R.B. SCOTT	BUCK
W.R. REYNOLDS	FRANK
LOUIS GRINNELL,	CHARLEY TIMOOK
Interpreter	TO-NAG

Now, therefore, be it known that I, ULYSSES S. GRANT, President of the United States of America, do, in pursuance of the advice and
consent of the Senate, as expressed in its resolution of the twenty-sixth
of June, one thousand eight hundred and sixty-six, accept, ratify, and
confirm the said Treaty, with the amendment aforesaid.

In testimony whereof, I have hereto signed my name, and have
caused the seal of the United States to be affixed.

Done at the city of Washington, this twenty-first day of October,
in the year of our Lord one thousand eight hundred and sixty-nine, and
of the Independence of the United States of America the ninety-fourth.

U.S. GRANT

By the President:
HAMILTON FISH
Secretary of State.

An Outline of Western Shoshone History

FIRST INCURSIONS

Since time immemorial, the Western Shoshone people have
lived in a symbiotic relationship with Newe Sogobia, a Great Basin
expanse that includes the eastern half of Nevada and stretches up
into Idaho and southwest into Death Valley. In the Shoshone
language, *Newe* means the people; *Sogobia* is the word for Mother
Earth. Hunters and gatherers with an intimate knowledge of the
fragile diverse life of this arid region, the Western Shoshone maintained a sustainable way of life with a strong tradition of respect for
the Earth.

In the 1820s, the first whites arrived in Newe Sogobia: they
were fur trappers and nearly succeeded in making beaver extinct in
the region. In the 1840s, migrants to the gold fields of California and
arable lands of Oregon began to pass through Newe Sogobia along
the Humboldt River, devastating the land they passed over and often
shooting the native peoples they saw out of fear and prejudice.
Occasionally, the Shoshone fought back in defense of their land,
food sources and lives. During those early years, the native grasses
and pinon pines were devastated, the waters polluted, the game
exterminated.

FROM TREATY TO RESISTANCE

Gold and silver from Nevada funded the Union side of the Civil
War, and so in 1863 the U.S. negotiated a treaty to protect the
transport routes. In this treaty of peace and friendship, the Treaty of
Ruby Valley, the Western Shoshone agreed to cease war against the
U.S. and to allow construction of railroad and telegraph lines, mines

and ranches. The treaty is distinct from those signed by most native nations with the U.S. in that it cedes no land to the U.S.; instead the Western Shoshone are repeatedly referred to as a nation, and the boundaries of this large nation described. Nothing in the treaty gave, ceded, sold or traded land to the U.S.

> *We all want to stay here . . . allowed to live in our own dear*
> *Mountains and Valleys as we have done in times gone. . . .*
> *We have been born and raised here; the Mountains and Valleys,*
> *with their Springs and Creeks, are our Fathers and Brothers.*
> —Statement of the Shoshones of east-central Nevada, 1873

The Bureau of Indian Affairs immediately began pressuring the Shoshone to give up their nomadic hunting and gathering lifestyles and adopt white farming and ranching methods. At the same time, white settlers harrassed the native people, driving them from their lands and burning their crops. Many killings and a few massacres took place in those hard years when the food sources had nearly vanished and new diseases ravaged the population. Traditional culture, language, and extended families or bands survived, however.

> *Permit me to say that the Shoshonees are annually suffering*
> *from the encroachments of white men. The miner is gradually*
> *penetrating their mountains from the north, from the east, and from*
> *the west in search of wealth. He is closely followed by the farmer,*
> *the speculator, and the adventurer who drive the Indian from his*
> *home and his country. . . .*
> —A.F. White, State Supt. of Public Instruction for Nevada, 1866

The U.S. had immediately violated the Treaty of Ruby Valley by giving and selling huge amounts of land to railroad companies and settlers and failing to deliver the goods that were supposed to compensate for devastation of land and food sources. In the early twentieth century, Western Shoshone leaders had already begun pressing for observation of the treaty and justice for their people. In 1934 the U.S. government passed the Indian Reorganization Act (IRA) which allowed it to install tribal leaders more answerable to their sponsors than their people. Many traditional people refused to recognize the new tribal governments, and the IRA left a legacy of divisiveness that plagues native nations into the present.

> *The Western bands of Shoshones have never parted with its*
> *right in areas of country recognized as belonging to it by the treaty*
> *of 1863 . . . the consequence is the Western bands of Shoshones*

*have never parted with and still have claim of right to hunt over
and occupy the area of country recognized as belonging to them by
treaty.*

—Western Shoshone leaders,
December 24, 1949

THE WESTERN SHOSHONE AND
U.S. BUREAUCRACY AFTER WW II

In 1946 the Indian Claims Commission (ICC) was established by
Congress to hear and resolve claims arising from U.S. taking of
indigenous nations' lands. But the federal courts immediately
interpreted the ICC's mission as solely that of compensating for
taken land, not restoration of the land. Attorneys representing
claimants were awarded 10% of monetary settlements, providing an
incentive for them to seek money rather than return of land.

The Bureau of Indian Affairs approved a claims contract between the law firm of Ernest Wilkinson, whose firm had helped
author the ICC's enabling legislation, and the IRA Temoak Band of
Western Shoshone, which was asserted to be the sole representative
of the large and widely scattered Shoshone Nation. The case crept
through the ICC system for decades. In 1962 the ICC concluded that
it "was unable to discover any formal extinguishment" of Western
Shoshone land title, but ruled that the lands were taken at some
point in the past. By 1966, Wilkinson and the U.S.'s lawyers arbi-
trarily stipulated that the extinguishment of Western Shoshone title
to over 22 million acres of land in Nevada had taken place on July 1,
1872. They determined that the amount of money owed to the
Western Shoshone would be determined by the value of Nevada land
in 1872, without interest, and minus the value of the few treaty
goods delivered in the 1860s and 1870s. *At this point, the ICC was
no longer interpreting history, but inventing it. No taking happened
in 1872 either on paper or on the land.* By 1976 virtually all Western
Shoshone bands agreed that the ICC and Wilkinson did not represent
their desire to have their land rights recognized, not extinguished.
Ultimately even the Temoak band attempted to fire Wilkinson, but
the BIA prevented them.

—Source: Western Shoshone Defense Project

The Great Basin Environment,
the Western Shoshone, and the U.S. Government

IN THE BEGINNING

The Western Shoshone nation covers much of the Great Basin—so called because this expanse of sagebrush country between the Rockies and the Sierras doesn't drain into any ocean. A fragile environment with little rainfall, the Great Basin is host to many rare and endangered species—the desert tortoise, bighorn sheep, antelope, lahontan cutthroat trout, beaver, as well as coyotes, mule deer, jackrabbits, migratory waterfowl, raptors, and many other species. Non-natives have frequently regarded this subtle, beautiful landscape as barren, worthless, or empty, and federal policy from the beginning through the present day reflects this hostile misunderstanding of the Great Basin.

The first whites to come to the Great Basin were fur-trappers who rendered beaver nearly extinct in the area by the 1830s. Great Basin buffalo too have vanished. Few whites settled in Western Shoshone territory, though prospectors came and went, leaving many ghost towns, slag heaps, and ore-refining toxics behind them. In 1864, a year after the U.S. and the Western Shoshone Nation signed a treaty of peace and friendship, a Nevadan reported,

"The game of the mountains and valleys are being frightened away by the appearance of the white man in this wild region, and the continual crack of his unerring rifle. The pine nut trees are rapidly being cut down and used for building purposes or fuel. The bunch grass, the seed of which formerly supplied the Indians with one of their chief articles of food, and which abounds in the Humboldt country, now fails to yield even the most scanty harvest

owing to its being eaten off as fast as it sprouts by the vast amounts
of stock which had been brought to the country by the settler. . . .
Thus you will see that the means of subsistence for the Indians of
this section for the past year and for the whole future, have been
greatly impaired if not completely destroyed."

UPROOTING NATIVE WAYS AND SPECIES
AS FEDERAL POLICY
At this time the U.S. Government through its Indian agents
began urging and forcing the native peoples of the Great Basin to
take up ranching and farming—though much of this land of little
rain is unsuitable to agriculture without massive irrigation. The
nomadic life of the people was seen as uncivilized rather than as a
superb adaptation of the widely scattered resources and delicate
balances of the land. The Treaty of Ruby Valley specified, "Whenever the President of the United States shall deem it expedient for
them to abandon the roaming life, which they now lead, and become
herdsmen or agriculturalists, he is hereby authorized to make such
reservations for their use within the country above described." In
fact, the reservations specified were not created, and few Shoshone
could be persuaded to resettle from the lands they knew and cared
for.

"The U.S. government carried out no part of the treaty with the
exception of distributing minor trinkets. . .and the 400 to 500 cattle
which the government gave to the Indians and subsequently took
away from them."
—Edna Patterson, Louise Ulph, Victor Goodwin,
Nevada's Northeast Frontier, 1969

Well into the twentieth century, native Nevadans were harrassed and driven off the land they attempted to ranch, and denied
access to the land base that would allow them to continue their
previous way of life in peace. In the case of the Dann Sisters, The
Bureau of Land Management (BLM) continues to try to force Western
Shoshone ranchers off the land. Meanwhile, the replacement of
indigenous plants with non-native ones begun by the emigrants of
the mid-nineteenth century was accelerated as official policy by the
BLM after World War II. Eighty-two percent of Nevada is considered
to be federal land, much of it under the jurisdiction of this bureau,
which has enormous impact on the environment as a whole. In the
1960s and 1970s, the BLM practiced plowing, spraying and "chaining"—all to accelerate the replacement of native species by grazing
fodder. (Chaining is done by dragging a 150-foot long, 90-pound per
link chain across the land with tractors; its primary purpose is to rip

out and destroy pinon pine—whose nuts are an important indigenous food source.) The herbicide 2-4-D, which was also used in Vietnam, was used on some sagebrush areas. Meanwhile, the BLM began to attempt to charge native peoples for gathering what pinon nuts remained after a century of abuse and attack.

FIGHTING A WAR AGAINST THE LAND

One of the most serious postwar threats to the Great Basin is the growth of the U.S. military in the West. Currently nearly 20% of all U.S. military land is in Nevada, including bombing ranges, laser and supersonic boom test ranges, experimental aircraft and tank practice grounds, and nuclear testing grounds. At the Bravo 20 Range in central Nevada, the BLM looked aside as the U.S. Air Force bombed lands considered public under U.S. law and sacred in Paiute tradition for over thirty years. The Western Shoshone's Newe Sogobia has been described as the most bombed nation on Earth: today tens of thousands of veterans who were intentionally exposed, "downwinder" civilian victims of radioactive fallout, and uncounted plant and animal deaths continue to result from nuclear testing.

The Western Shoshone National Council has been active in working with Nevada-based peace and environmental groups against testing and the other nuclear assaults on Nevada. During the 1970s and early '80s, the U.S. planned to base its mobile MX missile system in the Great Basin lands of Utah and Nevada, making them a "national sacrifice area" that would absorb vast quantities of Soviet nuclear missiles, according to the then-current cold war scenario.

Throughout the 1980s and into the present, the Western Shoshone have also been active in opposing nuclear testing and the development of a massive high-level waste dump near the Test Site at Yucca Mountain. Yucca Mountain, which holds an important place in Western Shoshone culture, is a seismically unstable, geologically and hydrologically complex site widely considered unsuitable for nuclear waste disposal. The Department of Energy continues to press for its opening as a permanent storage site for all U.S. high-level waste. The waste would remain highly dangerous for more than ten thousand years, radioactive for more than one hundred thousand years.

GIVING AWAY GOLD, GOUGING OUT THE GROUND

Since the Comstock Lode was discovered in the 1860s, mining has been one of Nevada's principal industries. Northeast Nevada is currently in the midst of a gold rush—more than 60% of U.S. gold production is in Nevada, and nearly half of that in the northeast quadrant of the state. Contemporary mining operations work with ore that earlier technologies and gold prices made infeasible to extract. Most mines are open pit mines in which whole mountains, landscapes and valleys are dug up, leached, and dumped. Gold is usually extracted with a cyanide solution which is then left in vast ponds to break down: Earth Island Journal reported the death of more than 9000 waterfowl from these poisonous ponds. Although fines for cyanide-caused wildlife deaths are high, the BLM allows mines to self-police their impact on wildlife. Some mines operating below the water table simply pump out thousands of gallons per minute, with ultimately unknown effect on the long-term water sources of their region. The BLM requires mines to have a "reclamation" plan, but thousands of acres of pitted, gouged land will clearly never be the same again.

GRAZING
　　The Bureau of Land Management was created in 1946 out of the merger of the Grazing Service with the General Land Office, and administering grazing on public land is still a principal task. Like the U.S. Forest Service, however, the Nevada BLM spends far more money on accommodating and administrating use than it takes in from fees. Meanwhile the BLM has been attempting to shift the focus of its long-running conflict with Carrie and Mary Dann from land ownership to grazing, possibly in an attempt to split the environmental and land-rights communities. Despite evidence established in court to the contrary, Nevada BLM director Billy Templeton has recently begun claiming that the reason the BLM continues to harrass these two Western Shoshone sisters is out of concern for the environment, even going so far as to suggest he would desist if they weren't damaging the range. Northern Nevada has been severely affected by the drought that has also plagued California for several years, but the Danns have reduced their herds well below the number they formerly grazed and the BLM agreed were okay during abortive negotiation meetings. Like the Danns, many Western Shoshone have refused to pay grazing fees to the BLM on the grounds that the Bureau has no right to administrate their land. The Western Shoshone National Council has set up a Wild Horse Management Program. In 1990, they conducted a roundup of 117 horses in an area where the drought-damaged range was suffering from overgrazing and waterhole damage while the horses were suffering from starvation and thirst. More recently, the BLM brought charges against WSNC chief Raymond Yowell and three other Western Shoshone activists for another wild horse roundup. Apparently the BLM will neither let the Western Shoshone graze their land, nor prevent it from being overgrazed. Examining the historical record, federal policy toward the Western Shoshone and the Great

Basin appears to be one of exploitation, short-term planning, misunderstanding and outright destruction of the land, and continual sabotage of any attempt at land-based livelihood for the people.

> *"Our work to maintain or regain environmental quality within our homelands is a facet of a wider, more complex jurisdiction over our territories and lives, and to protect our indigenous rights. As a nation, our rights are not derived from the U.S. Constitution or granted by any treaties; they existed prior to the United States' creation. As with other North American indigenous nations, the Western Shoshone's identity, purpose, and strength is based on our relationship to our homeland. . . . The ongoing struggle of the Western Shoshone is to protect our unrelinquished rights to our homelands, to preserve the environmental integrity of our territory, and above all, to fulfill the basic instructions given to us when we were newly created on Newe Sogobea."*
> —Joe Sanchez, Western Shoshone activist and environmentalist

Source: Western Shoshone Defense Project, 9/92

Western Shoshones Protest Nuclear Testing on Their Lands

by Judy Wells

More than fifteen hundred peace activists from around the world joined members of the Western Shoshone nation at the Nevada Test Site on April 3-8, 1991, to protest nuclear weapons testing at the site, which is illegally located on sovereign Shoshone lands. Organized by the Western Shoshone National Council and several grassroots activist groups, the six-day event included teach-ins, ceremonies, rallies, and nonviolent civil disobedience actions that resulted in more than 650 arrests.

From a flatbed truck equipped with loudspeakers, Western Shoshone leader Raymond Yowell said, "We're here to show our displeasure for what's going on. It's not good for health. It's not good for land. It's certainly against our religion." Western Shoshone elder Corbin Harney led protesters in a ceremony honoring Mother Earth. Later, he and Yowell were the first to be arrested during the event.

Hopi spiritual leader Thomas Banyacya conducted a workshop on the problems nuclear toxins are causing for humans and wildlife worldwide. "Every time they test, they kill millions of people in the next generation," he said.

During the last forty years, the Nevada Test Site area has been rocked and jarred by over seven hundred nuclear explosions, both above ground and below. Radiation has contaminated soil, air, and groundwater in the area; cancers and physical deformities are appearing at alarming rates in people and animals living near the test site. The devastation is an incomprehensible sacrilege to Shoshones who revere the Earth as Mother.

So far, however, the Shoshones have been unable to prevent the nuclear explosions, despite the fact that they have never sold or ceded their lands to the U.S., nor have they ever granted permission to test bombs there. President Harry Truman seized the land by executive order in 1951, in direct violation of the 1863 Treaty of Ruby Valley between the Shoshones and the U.S.

The Ruby Valley treaty guaranteed the Shoshones rightful ownership of their land in return for granting the U.S. safe passage for stagecoach, railway, and telegraph lines, and permission to establish military posts, mines, farms, and ranches in Shoshone territory. Although the Shoshones have honored the bargain, the U.S. has violated it many times. Since the treaty was signed, the U.S. government has placed nearly ninety percent of Shoshone lands under the control of governmental departments, including the Department of Energy, claiming that the lands were needed for national defense, conservation projects, recreation, and profit-making ventures.

For forty years, Shoshone people have been fighting an uphill battle to regain control of their lands. A decade ago, non-Shoshone anti-nuclear activists began supporting the Shoshones, and the Nevada Test Site has since become a focal point for the U.S. peace movement and campaign against nuclear testing.

In 1986, the Western Shoshone National Council introduced a new strategy in its struggle. Operating on the premise that only Shoshone people can legally grant or deny access to Shoshone land, the council began issuing anti-nuclear activists permits allowing them onto Western Shoshone land at the test site—knowing that facility officials would have the activists arrested as "trespassers." In challenging such arrests, the council contends that the U.S. government cannot convict people of trespassing on land that it doesn't own. So far, the tactic has been working. Charges of trespass have been consistently dropped.

In issuing the permits, the council has stated, "The Western Shoshone nation is calling upon citizens of the United States, as well as the world community of nations, to demand that the United States terminate its invasion of our lands for the evil purpose of testing nuclear bombs and other weapons of war. We must have your political help because we are militarily unable to resist the United States."

The Shoshone plea for help has resulted in a groundswell of response from citizens worldwide. Large-scale demonstrations are now held frequently at the site.

Participants in the action included representatives of indigenous nations from around the world that have suffered devastating effects from nuclear testing in their homelands. Also included were representatives of anti-nuclear organizations, such as the National Association of Radiation Survivors; Downwinders (people living downwind from the test site who have suffered effects of its radiation); Alliance of Atomic Veterans (soldiers who were intentionally exposed to radiation); and activists from anti-nuclear movements in Tahiti, the Marshall Islands, Japan, the USSR, and Europe.

As the U.S. government continues to block international attempts to establish a worldwide ban on nuclear weapons testing, peace activists are intensifying their campaigns to stop the tests and have scheduled demonstrations on a regular basis at the Nevada Test Site.

The Hundredth Monkey, another grassroots organization, is hoping to draw hundreds of thousands of global citizens to Nevada in an effort to stop nuclear testing at the test site through worldwide media exposure, political pressure, direct action, and prayer. They also hope to effect a return of the land to the Western Shoshone nation.

Submitted by Judy Wells, in *Shaman's Drum*, Summer, 1991. Sources: Literature from the American Peace Test, The Hundredth Monkey, and the Western Shoshone Nation; Test Banner, Winter/ Spring, 1991; Las Vegas Review Journal, April 7, 1991. Thanks to Marie Loren, Willits, CA.

Death and Healing in Newe Sogobia
The Nevada Nuclear Test Site—What's Going On?

by Mark Dyken

Newe Sogobia, the most bombed nation on the planet. You can't find this country on any maps—yet it has been inhabited and cared for by the same people for thousands of years.

Newe Sogobia is the Western Shoshone ancestral nation that encompasses most of the state of Nevada. The United States seized the land now known as the United States Nuclear Weapons Test Site, in violation of the Ruby Valley Treaty of 1863, and has been testing nuclear and other bombs on this sacred ground. Since 1951 over 900 nuclear explosions have taken place above and below the ground.

There are many sad faces to this story, including the hundreds of thousands of veterans who were knowingly exposed to deadly radiation who are now suffering and dying while the Veterans Administration refuses to acknowledge the connection between their exposure and their illnesses. The families of these victims, especially their children, are suffering and dying from various types of cancer and birth defects. There is no way of knowing how many generations down the line will be affected.

Down-winders across the country are also suffering, especially in Nevada where between 1978 and 1984 lung cancer rates among men was 31% above the national average. The rate for Nevada women was 53% above the national average. Child leukemia, brain tumors and cancers of the central nervous system, prostate, bladder, tongue and bone are all above the national average in Nevada.

The cost to the earth, plants, animals, air and water is impossible to figure. The radioactive contamination is far reaching and will last for thousands of years. The land is decimated with craters and blown-apart mountains. Chief Raymond Yowell of the Western Shoshone nation has commented that the only comparison he could make to explain how nuclear testing felt to his people was to ask, "How would you feel if someone put a bomb into your mother and blew it off?"

All the countries with nuclear capabilities test their weapons on the lands of native peoples. The Soviet Union test in Kazakhstan and Navaja Zembla; China tests on the lands of the Uygur; France tests on the coral islands in Polynesia; Great Britain first bombed Australian Aboriginal land and now joins the United States in testing on Western Shoshone land.

Corbin Harney is the spiritual leader of the Western Shoshone Nation. At an early age, when the U.S. government was working hard to destroy the Western Shoshone way of life with methods such as taking native children and putting them through public schools, prohibiting by law the Sundance and sweat lodge, and discouraging use of the native language, Corbin was taken away by elders to learn the old ways.

He is now one of the few members of his tribe who can speak and understand the native Shoshone language. He knows the sacred songs and medicine that were handed down through the generations. He has vision and communication with the Earth like no other person. Corbin looks like a part of his beloved, sacred desert, and in his ceremonies, song and prayer the desert lives and speaks. Right now there is no one to replace him. Unless someone steps forward soon, when he passes into the next world he will take all this knowledge with him and another culture will pass into extinction.

"You are The People now" is one of Corbin's favorite lines. He says it will take all of us to unite and heal the earth. He bestows blessings on gatherings at the Test Site in his native tongue and sings songs that can mesmerize people at a sunrise ceremony. Even though people don't know the language, they understand the songs.

Corbin has been arrested, along with other members of his tribe, several times at the test site and has mentioned stories of jail in the old days for doing the Sundance. Nowadays, his case never comes to court. It seems the U.S. federal government is not too excited about having him on trial for trespassing on his own peoples' land. Political avenues have never been open for native peoples and even civil disobedience doesn't bring a day in court, but the Shoshone man carries on the struggle for his people in the way he knows best—Spirit work. Playing the drum, singing the old songs, conducting sweat lodges, praying in his native tongue, doing his eagle dance, and speaking to people whenever he has the chance are some of the ways he weaves his healing.

People's Comprehensive Test Ban Treaty

Executed on March 31, 1990,
in Newe Sogobia (Western Shoshone Nation), Nevada Test Site

We, the People, Do Agree:

Article I: All nuclear states shall agree to end the conducting of or participation in any nuclear weapons test or other nuclear explosion. Any government that does not sign such an international agreement shall be condemned as a criminal violator of existing international agreements prohibiting crimes against humanity.

Article II: All nuclear testing facilities shall be closed and dismantled and control of the lands encompassing such facilities shall be returned to the indigenous people for peaceful purposes. Resources spent on testing shall be redirected to clean up and restore the land damaged by testing and to treat and compensate the people who have suffered health effects.

Article III: All information about the environmental and health effects of nuclear weapons testing and production shall be made public. An international non-governmental commission shall be formed to investigate the impact of nuclear weapons testing and production on health and the environment, to monitor nuclear waste sites, and to identify contaminated regions of the world.

Article IV: All peoples are responsible for taking such nonviolent action necessary to enforce the terms and conditions of this treaty. All peoples are further urged to organize coordinated nonviolent actions and demonstrations against nuclear weapons testing prior to and during the . . . International Comprehensive Test Ban Treaty Conference.

Lawsuits and Land Titles: The Present Situation

"The United States chose to leave these Indians where they were in the nineteenth century because the white man could see no value in their lands. The government simply forgot about them and never got around to stealing their lands. It now wishes to drive them off while pretending it happened a hundred years ago."
—John O'Connell, attorney for the Defense, U.S. v. Dann, 1991

Because the ICC had no independent authority to extinguish indigenous land title, a case involving two Western Shoshone women became a major test case for whether or not the aboriginal land rights had been extinguished. Known as U.S. v. Dann, the litigation began in 1974, when the Bureau of Land Management (BLM) charged the Dann sisters with trespass for grazing livestock on land claimed by the BLM. The Danns, as well as the Western Shoshone National Council, held that the BLM has no jurisdiction over Newe Sogobia and refused to apply for a grazing permit.

In a series of complex arguments and decisions, the federal courts disagreed with each other about whether title had been extinguished, and when. The U.S. v. Dann was spun out until 1980, when the district court decided that title had been good until December 12, 1979, the date the ICC closed the Temoak case with an award of $26 million for the supposed "taking," money still held by the Secretary of the Interior as trustee for the Western Shoshone (Native peoples are considered wards of the Secretary in many legal respects). Afterward, the courts suggested that although tribal title was decided, the Danns could argue a right based on "individual aboriginal title."

During the final court hearing in June of 1991, Mary and Carrie Dann rejected the concept of individual aboriginal title, jeopardizing their own livelihood to defend the Western Shoshone as a nation. The Danns believe that the rights of the Western Shoshone as a tribe or nation must not be allowed to be broken down to individual rights by the U.S. That summer, the BLM renewed the efforts it began in 1974, seeking court permission to confiscate the Dann's livestock and destroy their livelihood as ranchers. A powerful campaign of letter-writing to the BLM, the Secretary of the Interior and elected officials forced the BLM into negotiation that fall. The Western Shoshone National Council agreed to oversee the substantial reduction of Dann livestock on the open range in return for the BLM's promise to cancel plans to impound the livestock. The Danns reduced their cattle by 20% and horses by more than 75%.

Instead of continuing negotiations, however, BLM State Director Billy Templeton informed the WSNC that "use of the land planned by the Danns was in excess of what we could agree to. . .and that further dialogue on the subject would not be productive. "On February 8, the BLM staged a roundup of nearby wild horses as a media event, claiming to have begun impoundment of Dann livestock. But only some strays among the 161 mustangs bore a Dann brand. On April 10, the BLM and its contractors showed up again to round up Dann cattle. But Carrie Dann and non-violent activists who'd come to support the land rights struggle came out to meet them, and after a brief confrontation between the BLM agent and Carrie Dann, the cattle were released. During this period the BLM attempted to divide the environmental community from the Western Shoshone by making allegations that the Dann herds were overgrazing—a contention already satisfied in the courts. On July 29, the BLM renewed its "Notice of Intent to Impound." Meanwhile Western Shoshone National Council Chief Raymond Yowell and staffer Ian Zabarte were indicted on charges that they conducted an illegal roundup of wild horses in the Duckwater area. The roundup was not the first conducted by the WSNC in the region; after establishing a Wild Horse Management Program in 1990, they conducted a roundup of 117 horses in an area where the drought-damaged range was suffering from overgrazing and waterhole damage while the horses were suffering from starvation and thirst. On January 4, 1993, the Court ruled that the Western Shoshone presented "credible testimony" that a threat existed to reservation land and the roundup was necessary. Chief Yowell called the grand jury indictment "an offensive tactic brought by the United States Government to harass Western Shoshone leaders for resisting the attempts of the United States to remove Western Shoshone people from their lands." On March 26, the Western Shoshone National

Council nationalized the livestock belonging to Mary and Carrie Dann.

On November 19, 1992, over 30 armed federal agents entered the Dann Ranch area, completely blocking traffic both in and out. The nearby towns of Crescent Valley and Beowawe, Nevada were cordoned off to provide security for federal wranglers who were rounding up horses. A total of 262 horses were taken, 44 of which were Western Shoshone horses, the rest were wild horses that were either gathered in other areas or had strayed into the alotment through broken fences. Clifford Dann, brother to Mary and Carrie, was injured in trying to block the exit of confiscated horses. In protest to the theft of horses he dowsed himself with gasoline and threatened to ignite himself, declaring "By taking away our livestock you are taking away our lives." He was charged with assault on a federal officer. Clifford asserted Western Shoshone sovereignty and refused to testify or allow cross-examination of government witnesses. On May 17, 1993, Clifford was sentenced to nine months in prison, two years probation and a $5,000 fine on a conviction of interfering with a federal official in the performance of his duties.

The Western Shoshone National Council and the Western Shoshone Defense Project continue to move toward development of land management programs and other administrative functions of a sovereign government within the framework of the Creator's laws and have established a spiritual/cultural encampment near the Dann ranch. Senators and the European Parliament are taking a new look at the Western Shoshone land rights case. Efforts to reverse Clifford Dann's felony conviction continue. The Danns and their non-violent supporters continue to prepare against another roundup attempt or attempts to shut down the encampment. The U.S. continues nuclear testing, military maneuvers, overflights, bombings, licensing of massive open-pit gold mining operations, and destruction of cultural and sacred sites in Newe Sogobia.

Source: Western Shoshone Defense Project

New Gold Mine Threatens Western Shoshone Land

The Western Shoshone Defense Project and the Citizen Alert Native American Program are requesting supporters to help respond to the "Cortez Pipeline Gold Deposit" Draft Environmental Impact Statement. This lengthy document (400+ pages) recently released by the Battle Mountain District Bureau of Land Management describes the development of a new gold mine in Crescent Valley and its expected environmental impacts. Upon review of this document we feel that the proposed project will have serious effects on the environmental health of the area including the Dann sisters' traditional use lands.

WHAT IS THE PIPELINE PROJECT?
The Pipeline Project is a massive new gold mine to be located approximately 15 miles southwest of the Dann Ranch in Crescent Valley, Nevada. It would be owned and operated by the Cortez Joint Venture, a cooperative effort between mining multinationals Placer Dome and Kennecott. The Cortez Joint Venture currently operates the Cortez Gold mine and its associated facilities at the southern end of Crescent Valley. The proposed project includes the construction of a new processing mill capable of milling 5000 tons of ore a day, a 583-acre waste rock facility, a 420-acre combined heap leach and tailings facility, and a 240-acre, 1000 ft. deep open pit. This will likely be followed in the "reasonably foreseeable future" by a 233-acre expansion of the open pit, an additional 1019 acres of waste rock, and 532 acres of tailings. Furthermore, the mine must pump out the groundwater aquifer to reach the gold.

DEWATERING

The Pipeline Project intends to dewater at an initial rate of approximately 30,000 gallons per minute (gpm), annually pumping 49,000 acre ft. of groundwater. This water will be pumped into large, engineered ponds where it is supposed to reinfiltrate into the ground water table, based upon a two-year study by a private consulting firm, hired by Cortez Joint venture. According to this study by Woodward-Clyde there would be no "significant" impact to the surrounding springs and seeps.

We have many reservations about this process. First of all, this conclusion is based on a computer model which only predicts groundwater levels for a ten-year period. The initial life of the mine would be 12 years, and it is clear from the document that an additional 14 years of dewatering would result from southward expansions. The original Cortez Pit plans to begin dewatering in the reasonably foreseeable future. Thus, the predicted amount of pumping is severely underestimated.

Groundwater hydrology is so complex and difficult to predict, that any computer model is at best a gross simplification. At the Barrick Goldstrike Mine north of Crescent Valley, initial predictions set a pumping rate of 12,000 gpm. Currently, the mine has increased its pumping permit to allow almost 60,000 gpm, while rumors persist among employees that the true rate is perhaps closer to 100,000 gpm.

Pumping groundwater creates a cone of depression, lowering the water table and sucking other groundwater towards the center of the mining pit. . . .

Dewatering can also result in the ground subsiding, damaging the aquifer and permanently reducing its capacity to store water. At the Pipeline Project the ground is expected to sink as much as 20 inches in certain places, including beneath the proposed heap leach/tailings facility. Such sinkage increases the potential of ripping the plastic liner releasing toxic cyanide and heavy metals into the ground.

Upon completion of mining activities, the open pit would fill, creating a man-made lake. Evaporative groundwater loss from the pit lake and reinfiltration ponds would be permanent. There is also the potential for degradation of groundwater through the leaching of heavy metals in the pit walls. Water quality could be further reduced by leaks in the tailings impoundment and by acid mine drainage when moisture percolates through the waste rock dumps.

The Western Shoshone Defense Project feels that the Pipeline Project and its associated dewatering will have an effect on the long term environmental health of the region. In May of this year, the Western Shoshone Defense Project, the Western Shoshone National

Council, the Citizen Alert Native American Program and the Sierra Club participated in a joint press conference regarding dewatering.

Tom Meyers, hired by the Sierra Club to study the issue, found that the Humboldt River basin will face a serious water deficit in the future if dewatering continues. The fact that we have little understanding of dewatering's long term impacts was perhaps the most stunning finding of his report. Because of the furious rate at which the mines are proceeding with plans to dewater, the W.S.D.P. and C.A.N.A.P. demanded a cumulative impact study for the Humboldt River basin be undertaken before any new projects were to be permitted. Such a study had to include and respect Western Shoshone sovereign rights and responsibilities towards the water. Despite this demand the Bureau of Land Management has pressed forward with projects such as the Pipeline, ignoring their long term implications and cumulative impacts. . . .

MINING AND THE TREATY OF RUBY VALLEY
Article IV
It is further agreed by the parties hereto, that the Shoshone country may be explored and prospected for gold and silver, or other minerals; and when mines are discovered, they may be worked, and mining and agricultural settlements formed, and ranches established whenever they may be required. Mills may be erected and timber taken for their use, as also for building or other purposes in any part of the country claimed by said bands.

As illustrated in the above section of the Treaty of Ruby Valley, one of the rights granted to the U.S. by the Western Shoshone Nation was permission to mine on their lands. One might assume then that the proposed Pipeline Project is permitted under the Treaty. Yet, such an assumption is contrary to established treaty law. Treaties are agreements between sovereign, independent nations. At this time of the signing of the treaty (circa 1863), mining was conducted by the construction of shafts extracting visible veins of gold, or by panning visible granules found in stream beds. The Western Shoshone in no way agreed to the scale, intensity or form of modern open pit heap leach gold mining.

More importantly, the Treaty nowhere mentions water rights. It should be understood that these treaties do not give rights to Native Americans; they grant certain rights to the United States and its citizens. Those rights not specifically ceded in the document remain intact. As the original inhabitants of Newe Sogobia, the Western Shoshone retain their inherent rights and responsibilities towards the waters within their aboriginal territory. Thus the expropriation, exploitation, and removal of these waters as proposed by the Pipeline Project and other mines is in violation of the Treaty of

Ruby Valley and an infringement upon Western Shoshone sover-eignty.

"Water is the life blood, the key to the whole thing. Without water, our land rights struggles—even if we were to win back every square inch of our unceded lands—would be meaningless. With the water which is ours by aboriginal right, by treaty right, and by simple moral right, we Indians can recover our self-sufficiency and our self-determination. Without that water, we are condemned to perpetual poverty, erosion of our land base, our culture, our popula-tion itself. If we do not recover our water rights, we are dooming ourselves to extinction. It's that simple. And I say that the very front line of the Indian liberation struggle, at least in the plains and desert regions, is the battle for control over our water."

—Madonna Thunderhawk, Hunkpapa Lakota,
Women of All Red Nations

Source: Jennifer Viereck, Healing Global Wounds, P.O. Box 13, Boulder Creek, CA 95006.

Yucca Mountain Unsafe for Storage of Nuclear Waste

In 1987 legislators established the Office of the Nuclear Negotiator under the DOE. Its job was to find some place—preferably Indian land—to store the high-level, radioactive waste from 100 nuclear power plants scattered around the country in thirty states.

A new report, compiling the findings of independent geologists from the U.S. and abroad working under a Nevada Nuclear Projects Agency contract, concludes that minerals found on the surface of Yucca Mountain—the proposed high-level nuclear waste dump—were carried there by warm springs from under the mountain.

This report has grave implications for the government's plans to construct the waste dump at Yucca Mountain. If water rose through the mountain to the surface before, it could do so again; and if radioactive waste were entombed in the mountain, the water could flood the repository and spread the waste throughout the environment.

The new study confirms the position of former Yucca Mountain Project geologist Jerry Szymanski, who resigned from the Department of Energy in 1992 after the agency rejected his findings. While the current water table is substantially below the level of the proposed waste dump, Szymanski believes that earthquakes could cause warm water to squirt to the surface from deep within the earth's crust.

—Source: Citizen Alert, April 1994

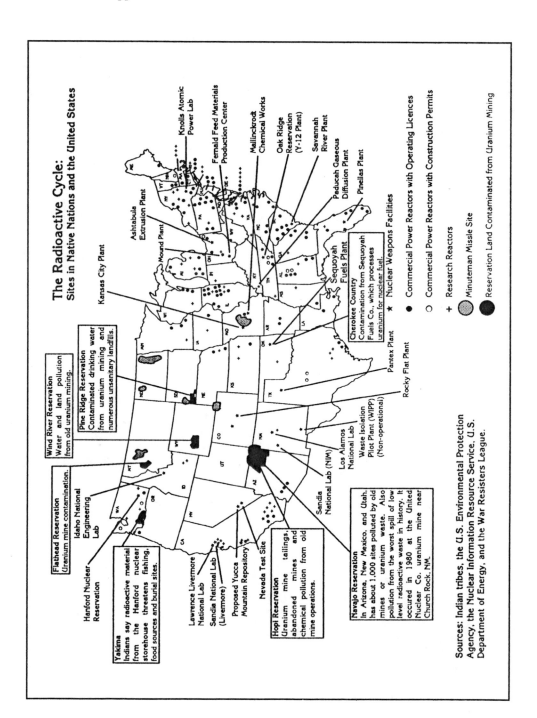

The Radioactive Cycle:
Sites in Native Nations and the United States

Sources: Indian tribes, the U.S. Environmental Protection Agency, the Nuclear Information Resource Service, U.S. Department of Energy, and the War Resisters League.

Scientists Fear Atomic Explosion of Buried Waste
Argument Strikes New Blow Against a Proposal
for a Respository in Nevada

by William J. Broad

Debate has broken out among Federal scientists over whether the planned underground dump for the nation's high-level atomic wastes in Nevada might erupt in a nuclear explosion, scattering radioactivity to the winds or into ground water or both.

The debate, set off by scientists at the Los Alamos National Laboratory in New Mexico, is the latest blow to the planned repository deep below Yucca Mountain in the desert about 100 miles northwest of Las Vegas. Opponents of nuclear power and Nevada officials have long assailed the project as ill-conceived and ill-managed, and it has encountered numerous delays.

Even if scientists can debunk the new argument that buried waste at Yucca Mountain might eventually explode, the existence of so serious a dispute so late in the planning process might cripple the plan or even kill it. Planning for the repository began eight years ago and studies of its feasibility have so far cost more than $1.7 billion. The Federal Government wants to open the repository in 2010 as a permanent solution to the problem of disposing of wastes from nuclear power plants and from the production of nuclear warheads.

The possibility that buried wastes might detonate in a nuclear explosion was raised privately last year by Dr. Charles D. Bowman and Dr. Francisco Venneri, both physicists at Los Alamos, the birthplace of the atomic bomb. In response, lab managers formed three teams with a total of 30 scientists to investigate the idea and, if possible, disprove it.

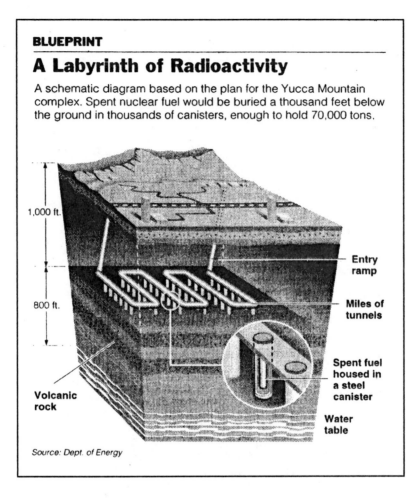

BLUEPRINT

A Labyrinth of Radioactivity

A schematic diagram based on the plan for the Yucca Mountain complex. Spent nuclear fuel would be buried a thousand feet below the ground in thousands of canisters, enough to hold 70,000 tons.

1,000 ft.

800 ft.

Entry ramp

Miles of tunnels

Spent fuel housed in a steel canister

Volcanic rock

Water table

Source: Dept. of Energy

While uncovering many problems with the thesis, the teams were unable to lay it to rest, laboratory officials say. So the lab is now making the dispute public in scientific papers and is considering having it aired at large scientific meetings as well. . . .

Highly radioactive wastes are the main orphan of the nuclear era, having found no permanent home over the decades. In theory, if the Yucca plan wins approval after a careful study of the area's geology, a labyrinth of bunkers carved beneath the mountain would hold thousands of steel canisters for 10,000 years, until radioactive decay rendered the wastes less hazardous.

The spent fuel from nuclear reactors is permeated with pluto-nium, which is a main ingredient used in making nuclear bombs.

Since plutonium 239 has a half-life of 24,360 years, significant amounts of it would remain active for more than 50,000 years, long after the steel canisters that once held the radioactive material had dissolved. (A radioactive substance's half-life is the period required for the disintegration of half of its atoms.)

With the end of the cold war, the Nevada site has increasingly been studied for a possible added role as a repository for the pluto-nium from scrapped nuclear arms. . . .

The most basic solution, Dr. Bowman said, would be removing all fissionable material from nuclear waste in a process known as reprocessing or by transmuting it in his proposed accelerator. Other possible steps would include making steel canisters smaller and spreading them out over larger areas in underground galleries—expensive steps in a project already expected to cost $15 billion or more.

A different precaution, Dr. Bowman said, would be to abandon the Yucca site, where the volcanic ground is relatively soluble. Instead, the deep repository might be dug in granite, where migra-tion of materials would be slower and more difficult. . . .

Dr. Daniel A. Dreyfus, the head of civilian radioactive waste management at the Energy Department in Washington, which runs Los Alamos and the Yucca Mountain studies, said he was keeping an open mind on whether Dr. Bowman's thesis might trigger an overhaul of the project. . . .

"Whether Yucca Mountain is the right site, I don't know. Maybe there's no good solution," he added. "But walking away from the problem is no solution either. We better keep trying, because we already made the decision to have the wastes in the first place."

Source: *New York Times*, 3-5-95.

Nuclear Waste Transportation

"With Yucca Mountain, Nevada, being named by Congress as the only site to be studied for disposal of the irradiated fuel from the nation's commercial nuclear power plants, the question of how this nuclear waste would be transported to Yucca Mountain becomes an important one for everyone in the nation. . . .

"Using Department of Energy information and route selection and analysis codes, along with specific reactor information, we have mapped the most likely highway and rail transport routes from each reactor location to Yucca Mountain. . . .

"This means the utilities' irradiated nuclear fuel could be moving on the nation's highways and rails three years from now (1998). We in Nevada have long been concerned about the safety of possible rail and highway routes to Yucca Mountain, not just in Nevada which currently has no rail access to Yucca Mountain, but from the 75 commercial reactor locations spread over 34 states."
—Source: Agency for Nuclear Projects,
Nuclear Waste Project Office, Carson City, NV, 2/95

Transportation of high-level nuclear wastes from reactor sites to proposed storage facilities is a pressing concern for all states. The U.S. Department of Energy could be transporting spent fuel and HLNW (high-level nuclear waste) on the nation's highways and railroads to Yucca Mountain, Nevada by 1998.

If a high-level nuclear waste dump opens in Nevada, up to 2,500 shipments per year of highly radioactive material will be moving along interstate highways and railroads.

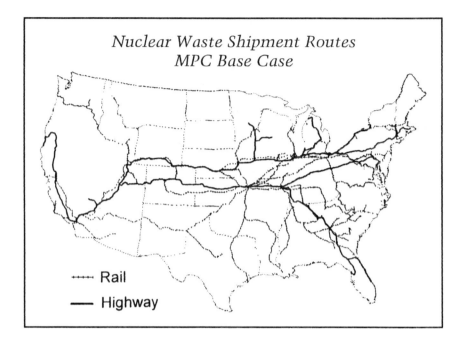

Nuclear Waste Shipment Routes
MPC Base Case

┄┄ Rail

— Highway

Waste will pass through densely populated cities like Los Angeles, Las Vegas, Albuquerque, Denver and Salt Lake City, and many others.

In a severe accident, radioactive waste will contaminate homes, neighborhoods, and major business centers *to a radius of 500 miles or more.* Is your local community prepared? Are there alternatives?

A FLOATING CHERNOBYL HEADING OUR WAY! PLUTONIUM WASTE BOAT LEAVES FRANCE FOR JAPAN

In 1992, 43 nations banned from their territorial waters the *Akatsuki Maru,* carrying 100 nuclear weapons worth of plutonium from France to Japan. Now Japan intends to transport ultra toxic plutonium wastes around the globe against the cry of en-route nations. The first of many planned shipments is expected to leave Cherbourg, France via the Panama Canal heading through the Pacific Ocean for Japan on February 23, 1995.

Opposition to the shipment continues to mount. The 13-country Caribbean Community Heads of Government meeting in Belize (2-17-95) issued a statement condemning the shipment of plutonium waste through the region. "We are particularly disturbed that, in spite of our previous condemnation of such hazardous traffic and the clear danger it poses to our region, this shipment continues to go forward."

—Source: the Pacific Plutonium Forum

"We strongly oppose this shipment, as the Japanese government is remarkably irresponsible in this shipment as a whole, and there are so many unresolved safety issues, and would threaten the whole world to a radioactive hazard. We urge all nations, including the countries prospected to be en route the shipment, to voice out concerns and protests to the governments of Japan, France, and the U.K."

—Source: Citizens' Nuclear Information Center, Tokyo, 2/16/95

Use, Re-use and Misuse of Radioactive Material

We are used to using our senses to distinguish the natural from the artificial, the safe from the dangerous. But now we face a new challenge—radioactive contamination—and the injuries it causes cannot be detected without a Geiger counter.

It is indeed a horrifying image: radioactive material not in its own special storage place, but in the walls of your own home and in the steel products you use in your daily life.

The disasters were discovered by coincidence and no one can say "I'm safe" without tests and checks. We are all more at risk than workers in nuclear power plants who know what they are up against.

Yes—natural resources have to be recycled, but recycling radioactively contaminated material turns out to be most dangerous, damaging, and costly.

At all stages of the economic cycle there is the danger of exposure to radiation. In the production sector, radioactive material and processes are being used even in environments thought to be safe, like food processing; stereo, audio, and computer component manufacturing; public and private construction. In the consumption sector, irradiated products are being discovered all the time, for example, indoor window frame, fittings, and manhole covers. In the recycling sector, small amounts of contaminate waste irradiate large amounts of scrap and endanger unsuspecting workers in scrap yards and ports.

In April 1994, The Baton Rouge newspaper, *The Advocate,* reported on three major oil companies which found a way to dispose of a thorny problem: radioactive oil-field equipment, by selling the contaminated equipment as scrap to China, where it is melted down for reuse.

On August, 1994, it was announced in Beijing that Chinese scrap metal traders had bought Ukraine nuclear-powered submarines. Cash-strapped Ukraine, spotting a hungry market, has exported large amounts of scrap to China at rock-bottom prices—some of it radioactive. And steel traders in Hong Kong have said that they imported millions of tons of scrap from the Ukraine, most of which is smelted down and used as building material.

Because of the considerable amount of radioactivity involved and the worldwide distribution of the contaminated products, only internationally coordinated efforts by government, producers, traders, and consumers will succeed in again making our living environments free of nuclear contamination.

Source: Nina Sato, Shirasuna-tyo 3-26-105, Mizuho, Nagoya 467, Japan, Phone & Fax 81-52-834-8272.

Western Shoshone Ongoing & Current Issues

* Resolving sovereign nation status and land rights issues under the 1863 Treaty of Ruby Valley

* Nuclear testing and nuclear waste transportation and storage on Shoshone lands in violation of the Treaty

* Interference with religious practices and cultural, social and ethnic customs

* Increased mining and water exploration on Shoshone treaty lands under the 1872 Mining Act (i.e., cheap "public" land purchases)

* Desecration of sacred sites and Shoshone burial grounds (e.g., Rock Creek)

* Large scale military operations carried out and further expansion planned (e.g., Duck Valley)

* Hazardous waste disposal and cyanide leach gold mining on treaty lands

* Illegal trespass and (theft) roundup of Shoshone livestock by BLM agents

Organizations / Addresses

Alliance of Atomic Veterans,
  P.O. Box 32, Tipock, AZ
  86436. 602-768-6623
American Peace Test,
  P.O. Box 225, Eugene, OR
  97440. 503-343-8548
  P.O.Box 26725, Las Vegas,
  NV 89126. 702-386-9834
Campaign 95, 803 North Main
  St., Goshen, IN 46526.
  219-534-3402,
  fax 219-534-4937
Campaign for
  the Non-Proliferaion Treaty,
  21 DuPont Circle, NW,
  Fifth Floor, Washington,
  D.C. 20036.
  202-223-5956, fax 785-9034
Citizen Alert, P.O. Box 5339,
  3680 Grant Drive, Reno, NV
  89513. 702-827-4200
Council for Renewable Energy
  Education, 1730 North Lynn
  Street, Suite 602,
  Arlington,VA 22209.
  703 522-5305

Critical Mass Energy Project,
  215 Pennsylvania Avenue
  SE, Washington D.C. 20003.
  202-546-4996
CTB Clearinghouse,
  1819 "H" St., NW, Ste. 640,
  Washington, D.C. 20006-
  3603. 202-862-9740 ext.
  3051, fax 202-862-9762
Energy Conservation Coalition,
  1525 New Hampshire
  Avenue NW, Washington,
  D.C. 20036. 202-75-4874
Environmental Defense Fund,
  5655 College Avenue, Suite
  304, Oakland, CA 94618.
  415-658-8008
Foundation for a Compassionate
  Society, P.O. Box 868, Kyle,
  TX 78640. 512-268-1415
Friends of the Earth, 218 D St.
  SE, Washington, D.C.
  20003. 202-544-2600
Greenpeace USA, 1436 "U" St.,
  NW, Washington, D.C.
  20009. 202-319-2554,
  fax 202-462-4507

The Hundredth Monkey, P.O.
Box 402, Arcata, CA95521.
707-826-2641

Institute for Energy and
Environmental Research,
6935 Laurel Ave.,
Takoma Park, MD 20912.
301-270-5500

Institute for Peace Science,
Hiroshima University,
1-1-89 Higashisendamachi,
Hiroshima 730, Japan.
fax 81 82 245-0585

International Association of
Lawyers Against Nuclear
Arms, P.O. Box 11589,
2502 AN The Hague,
Netherlands.
31 70 363-4484,
fax 31 70 345-5951

International Network of
Engineers and Scientists for
Global Responsibility,
P.O. Box 101707,
44017 Dortmund, Germany.
49 231 721-7158,
fax 49 231 721-7159

International Peace Bureau,
41 Rue de Zurich,
1201 Geneva, Switzerland.
41 22 731-6429,
fax 41 22 738-9419

International Physicians for the
Prevention of Nuclear War,
126 Rogers Street,
Cambridge, MA 02142-
1096. 617-868-5050,
fax 617 868-2560

The Lawyers' Committee on
Nuclear Policy,
666 Broadway, Suite 625,
New York, NY 10012.
212-674-7790,
fax 212 674-6199

Nevada Desert Experience,
P.O. Box 4487, Las Vegas,
NV 89127. 702-646-4814

Nuclear Information and
Resource Service, 1424 16th
Street NW, Suite 601,
Washington, D.C. 20036.
202-328-0002

NukeWatch, P.O. Box 2658,
Madison, WI 53701.

Peace News, 5 Caledonian Road,
London N1 9DX, England.
44 71 278-3344,
fax 44 71278-0444

Plutonium Free Future, 2018
Shattuck Ave. Box 140,
Berkeley, CA 94704.
510-540-7645, fax 540-6159

Public Citizen,
215 Pennsylvania Ave. SE,
Washington, D.C. 20003.
202-546-4996

Oregon PeaceWorks, 333 State
St., Salem, OR 97301.
503-585-2767

Peace Action, 1819 H St. NW,
Suite 640, Washington, D.C.
20006. 202-862-9740,
fax 862-9762

Renew America,
1001 Connecticut Avenue
NW, Suite 719, Washington,
D.C. 20036. 202-466-6880

Rocky Mountain Institute,
1739 Snowmass Creek
Road, Old Snowmass, CO
81654. 303-927-3851

Safe Energy Communication
Council,
1717 Massachusetts Ave.,
NW Suite 805, Washington,
D.C. 20036. 202-483-8491

Shundahai Network,
    507 P Street NW,
    Washington, D.C. 20001.
    202-588-0912
Swedish Engineers for Nuclear
    Disarmament, Box 163655,
    S-103 27, Stockholm,
    Sweden.
War and Peace Foundation,
    32 Union Square East,
    New York, NY 10003.
    212-777-4210,
    fax 212 995-9652
Western Shoshone Defense
    Project, General Delivery,
    Crescent Valley, NV 89821.
    702468-0230, fax 468-0237
Western Shoshone National
    Council, P.O. Box 140115,
    Duckwater, NV 89314-0115.
    702-863-0332

Western States Legal
    Foundation, 1440 Broadway,
    Suite 500, Oakland, CA
    94612. 510-839-5877,
    fax 510-839-5397
World Court Project,
    67 Summerheth Rd.,
    Hailsham, Sussex BN27
    3DR England.
    44 0323 844 269
World Disarmament Campaign
    UK, 45-47 Blythe Street,
    London E2 6LX.
    44 71 729-2523
Worldwatch Institute, 1776
    Massachusets Avenue NW,
    Washington, D.C. 20036.
    202-452-1999

Video copies of Corbin Harney's 40-minute PBS program,
"One Water. One Air. One Earth." may be ordered from
Idaho Public Television, 1455 N. Orchard, Boise, ID 83706.
Phone: 208-373-7220, 800-543-6868.

Correspondence to the author and tax-deductible donations
may be sent to support Corbin Harney's work.
Corbin Harney
c/o Shundahai Network
Poo-Ha-Bah
P.O. Box 187, Tecopah, CA 92389
760-852-4288

For Corbin's tour and speaking schedule, please call Blue Dolphin,
530-265-6925.

Index

Note: page references in italics refer to illustrations.

Poo-Ha-Bah Healing Center

My family has been healers from the beginning, that is part of my blood, and I can't get away from it. For many years, my people have been coming to me and asking me to work on them. Working on people is a very important part of my life, because I was put on this earth to pray for people.

For a long time, I have wanted to set up a Healing Center. I have looked at many hot springs around the country for the Healing Center. Many of them have lost their power. I have chosen a very good place in Tecopa, California (near Las Vegas, Nevada). My people have used these springs for many, many generations.

The water is very important. This hot water can heal a lot of sickness—arthritis, bone aches—and with me working with this water, praying for people, it would give the Water Spirit that much more strength. And it will give me strength to continue at the same time.

Poo-Ha-Bah means "doctor waters," or "medicine waters." The Poo-Ha-Bah Healing Center can make my work easier, for the people I have been working on for many years now, by being able to put them in the water, and the same thing in the mud. Because I have seen how the Nature works.

We have to continue to ask the Nature to heal us from our sickness. That's what the healing water is there for. The Creator has put it there for us to use. That's what the people have used for thousands and thousands of years.

I would like to see the people help one another and come there to the healing water. So we'll be together praying, so the Spirit of the water can hear us, so in turn the Spirit of the water can heal us.

—Corbin Harney, July 1999

For additional information:
Poo-Ha-Bah
P.O. Box 187 • Tecopa, CA 92389 • (760) 852-4288

Printed in the United States
17645LVS00005B/28-36

9 780931 892806